Financial Forecasting in Microsoft® Excel

Financial Forecasting in Microsoft® Excel

Jeffrey Kenneth Prager

NAHB BuilderBooks.com

NAHB® National Association of Home Builders

Financial Forecasting in Microsoft® Excel

BuilderBooks, a Service of the National Association of Home Builders

Elizabeth M. Rich	Director, Book Publishing
Elizabeth M. Rich	Book Editor
D. V. Suresh	Cover Design
Electronic Quill Publishing Services	Composition
King Printing Company, Inc.	Printing

Gerald M. Howard NAHB Chief Executive Officer
Lakisha Woods, CAE NAHB Vice President, Publishing & Affinity Programs

Disclaimer

Printed in the United States of America.

18 17 16 15   1 2 3 4 5

ISBN: 978-0-86718-733-5
eISBN: 978-0-86718-734-2

Library of Congress CIP information available on request.

For further information, please contact:

National Association of Home Builders
1201 15th Street, NW
Washington, DC 20005-2800
800-223-2665
Visit us online at BuilderBooks.com

Contents

List of Figures and Tables

Figures

Tables

About the Author

Jeff Kenneth Prager is the Founder of Backroom Management Services. Backroom provides financial management (accounting, bookkeeping and consulting) services with an emphasis on the construction industry. They use CASHFLO™ which is their own proprietary web-based system that includes a robust accounting, estimating, scheduling and job costing system. Their focus is on management and growth. Their goal is to help you drive consistent and predictable cash flow.

Jeff has been a CPA, business owner and entrepreneur for over 35 years. He has been a former CEO/CFO and owner of several successful multimillion-dollar companies. He was one of the founders of Ashworth Golf Clothing, the CFO/partner of a large land development company and the owner of Strauss Homes, which was once rated as the second largest privately owned home builder in Colorado and in the top 100 privately owned companies of Colorado (2003). During his career, he has helped companies raise over $1 billion (of which $200 million was for his own companies). Jeff also served as an instructor of managerial economics (applying economic theory to business decisions) at the University of Colorado at Denver. Jeff has spoken at IBS and is a frequent contributor to NAHB Biztools and other publications of NAHB. He was published in the 2012 Cost of Doing Business Study and is a contributor to that study.

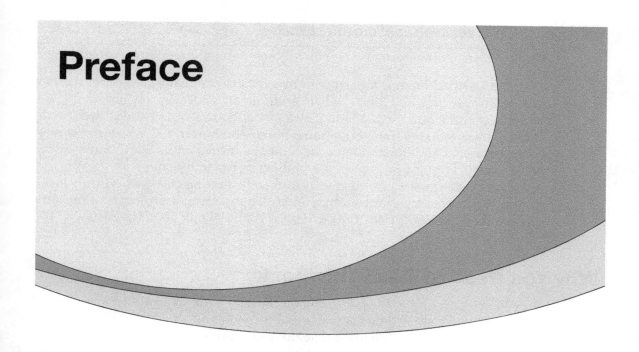

Preface

Apples, Apples, Apples!

In early 1980, as a vice president of finance for a real estate and investment firm, I had just received authorization to buy a micro-computer ($10,000 in 1980 dollars) that had no proven application or utility. It was state of the art with two ten-megabyte floppy drives. One floppy drive held the program, and the other the data. Everything was on the line. The president of the company walked in, looked at the computer screen, the manual next to the computer (yes, software came with manuals and tutorials, not help screens), and there I was learning to use VisiCalc (a precursor to Lotus which was a precursor to Excel).

I was typing Apples in cell A1, Apples in cell B5, and Apples in cell D3. The president just stared at me. "I just paid $10,000 for you to type in Apples?" he asked. Yes, he did. But within days I had formulas for amortization, industrial property, mixed-use properties, and partnership splits. When he showed my print-out to clients, it made deals that no one else could explain. I learned to tell stories with numbers, and that is what I intend to do in this book.

I got so good that a couple of people started their own ventures in real estate and promised me a guaranteed salary if I'd start my own CPA firm specializing in growing companies. In fact, by the time my practice was three years old, we had helped clients raise over $300 million.

Approximately 1985, a group contacted me to create a projection on a series of golf-driving ranges. When I input their numbers into the spreadsheets, it became obvious that their concept was flawed and was doomed to failure. The owners of the company (then called Charter Golf) asked me to take them down a different path focusing instead on golf clothing. Using the same skills, we crafted a projection based on specialty golf shirts. That company later became known as Ashworth Golf Clothing, and we ultimately went public.

In the 1990's, I became a partner in two companies involved in the real estate space. One was Strauss Homes, where I ultimately ended up owning the whole company, and the other was a land development company. Every deal was predicated on a projection. Ultimately, Strauss Homes built over 500 homes in the metro-Denver area. Our land development company owned mineral and water rights, and our single largest deal was an $80 million dollar transaction.

Please don't think I'm bragging! I'm merely sharing this with you to make a point: When you do a projection, you are approaching a project or a business with the "End in Mind," one of the 6 Success Factors I talk about in my book, *The Peddlers Son.*

Why You Need to Read This Book

Can you imagine a football team going on the field without a game plan? Absurd! Yet, many people go into business without a roadmap to success. The projection serves that purpose. The chances that the projections are absolutely correct are minimal. Then why do it? Because without benchmarks you will aimlessly move forward, and your business will control you instead of you controlling it! Some projections can be done on the back of a napkin; some involve serious assumptions like the ones that I will explain later in this book. Overall, I learned that no matter how complex the projections, you need to be able to explain them quickly.

The second thing I learned about projections is that they need to be flexible. I remember working on a hospital expansion during my tenure with Touche-Ross (one of the 'big eight' accounting firms now buried in the annals of Deloitte). We used 13-column green accounting paper (some of you may remember this) and had a projection for every major department that rolled up into a hospital summary sheet. When the manager of the job would change an assumption, I'd pull out my paper, pencil, and eraser. It would take hours upon hours to make a change. We had to erase the old numbers, put in the new and make sure that it carried through all the sheets. It was tedious. I'll bet I had three months of work into this one projection.

But, thanks to technology, we can write formulas that quickly change as assumptions change. What took days and weeks now takes milliseconds. Quite remarkable when you think about it! But the underlying thought process in a projection remains the same as when we did it by hand. Now it's my turn to pass on the secrets of successful projections to you.

And what's more, we can create sensitivity analyses whereby we can see the various returns on our investment given different investment criteria. This handles the objection "What if your rental rates are $0.90 per square foot instead of $1.25?" You just change the assumption, and viola! You can see the results.

The Four Questions

The purpose of a projection is to answer the following questions:

- How much money do you need?
- When do you need it?
- How and when will you repay the money?
- What is the risk?

These questions embody the essence of all business finance. Whether it's your own money, a bank's, or an investor's, these are the four questions you must ask when crafting a projection. Once you answer these questions, you are on your way. If you can't answer them to your own satisfaction, why would you consider making the investment?

Conventions

All of the spreadsheets, illustrations, and procedures refer to Microsoft® Excel 2010 for PC. Over time, there will be new functions and the visual effects may change, but the functionality and formulas will change very little.

Included with this book is a website that contains all the projections that we use throughout the book: www.nahb.org/financialforecasting. The files are arranged by chapter, so they are easy to navigate. You can go to the worksheets and copy and test those formulas through the Evaluate Formula dialog box.

In this book, we are not trying to show a comprehensive example, but expose you to the theory of programming in Excel.

Whenever I mention a formula, I will separate it from the sentence with a colon. If the formula ends in a quotation mark and it is a sentence, the period will be after the quotation mark. For instance, the formula to type is: **=Assumptions!A1&CHAR(10)&"Sales.**

When you go to enter a formula in Excel, type: **=Assumptions!A1&CHAR(10)& "Sales"**. Note the quotation marks around the word Sales, which is correct. In programming, syntax is everything. Syntax is the way the computer can interpret the command.

When we discuss the IF statements, there is normally a ")" at the end of the statement. Yet if you have nested IF statements, then you need a bracket for each IF statement. This may mean the end of an IF statement has several close parentheses , i.e.")))". Watch the brackets; they resemble the same order as brackets in those using algebra.

If you want to see how Excel calculates the components of a function or command, click on the **Formulas** tab and then Evaluate Formula (fig P.1). Once in that dialog box, click the **Evaluate** button (which leads you through the calculation), and it will show the results for each and every step in the formula.

Figure P.1 Evaluate Formula dialog box.

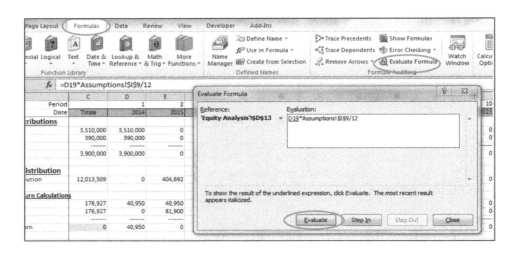

I could have also written this: **Formula** tab➔Evaluate Formula➔Evaluate.

Our Goal

When I retired in 2007, I found I was severely allergic to retirement. So, since 2008 I have been helping companies in driving predictable and consistent cash flow, as that is what ultimately leads to success. As I look back, that is what I've been doing throughout my entire career, whether they were companies of my own or not.

Through the use of transparent projections, I've helped companies raise over $1 billion in debt and equity; over $200 million was for companies I've owned. I worked hard to acquire this skill and through this book, I'm going to try to teach it you.

Acknowledgments

In advance, I'd like to thank my editors and the people who reviewed the content of this book before publication. That includes: Scott Stroud of Builder Radio, Noel Lane formally of Melody Homes (one of my most formidable competitors), Judy Prager (my wife and my inspiration) and countless people who let me create their projections for their projects.

A final acknowledgment goes to all the people who pose questions and those who gave answers on the Internet. When I learned VisiCalc and Lotus we only had books. Forums were a group of people who got together and discussed and solved problems. Although that had its social benefits the Internet is instant access to solutions and resources. While writing this book, I came across a lot of problems that I formally solved by brute force because it was "my projection." I probably learned more writing this book than you will by reading this book.

Introduction

Creating Projections

Cash flow is the constantly changing stream that is the source of all the financial (and much of the non-financial) data being collected. Before we create a projection, let's look at how cash flows through your organization. Regardless of the economic environment, you can predict short-term and long-term cash flow.

The Bucket Theory

Most business owners focus all their attention on generating profits. This is a mistake. When you broaden your focus to also include cash flow, you're on the way to building a company with consistent value—and in the long run, that's what really pays off.

Figure I.1 shows you how a business breathes. Instead of breathing air, it breathes money. Money comes in, and money goes out. Money (credit) comes from various sources such as sales from products and services (your normal operations), loans, owner contributions, and interest income, among other things.

The flow of cash (the water) makes its way into a general trough. Along the way, money goes out to support operations and expenses. Until the money starts coming in faster than it is going out and you create a "waterline" that is high enough, there is no cash available to pay *you*. You must monitor your cash at every point. The only time that you can really take money out of your business without killing it is when the money is coming in faster than it's going out.

Cash flow reflects financial needs for operational requirements and reserves for the unexpected. The cash forecast is a plan of cash receipts (money coming in) and cash expenditures (money going out) for a specific period of time, usually in monthly increments. There are three different types of cash flow:

Figure I.1 The bucket theory

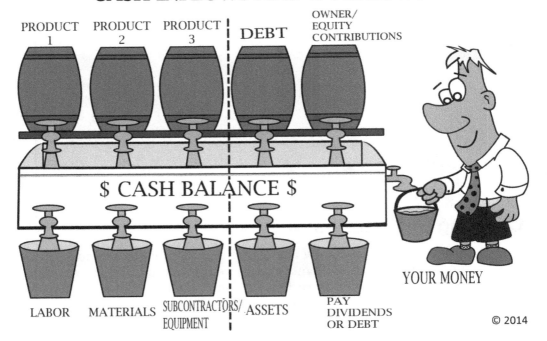

- Negative—Money goes out of your pocket faster than you can put it in your pocket.
- Breakeven—Money goes out of your pocket at the same rate as it enters your pocket.
- Positive—Money goes into your pocket faster than it goes out, leaving money for you!

The objective of a business is to create long-term, positive cash flow through operations.

Why Do I Need a Cash Projection?

Cash flow projections are essential for the following reasons:

- To assess project feasibility;
- To fund company cash needs, giving the company advance warning in which to plan and develop executive sensible borrowing programs;

- To determine financial feasibility of various programs or projects before commitments are made;
- To obtain funds *before* they're needed so they're available when needed;
- To identify problems before they become major. By comparing deviations of forecasted levels of cash with actual results, management is offered an opportunity to revise or react to unforeseen or uncontrollable developments;
- To open up opportunities by being in a better position to take advantage of cash discounts, make small-term investments, or take advantage of other opportunities to use liquid funds more profitably;
- To facilitate organizational alignment. Effective forecasting calls for an organized effort, cooperation of all non-financial executives, time, and energy.

Sources of information for cash projections are:
- Sales schedule
- Construction schedule
- Land development cost plan
- Overhead expense plan

Steps in Creating a Forecast

There are essentially eight steps in creating a forecast, and we will cover each step as we go through the book.

Step 1. Establish your objectives.

Step 2. Determine your cash inflows from sales.

Step 3. Schedule your costs of production.

Step 4. Budget your overhead costs.

Step 5. Determine other sources of funds.

Step 6. Determine what expenses you'll need to pay that aren't on your income statement.

Step 7. Determine your equity needs and the amount you will pay your investors.

Step 8. Do a postmortem on each project.

Step 1. Establish Your Objectives

This is usually profit oriented, but can include other objectives, such as conservation of capital, limitations on risk, and other sundry criteria.

Once you have looked at your historical results, determine a course of action. Define your goals (both financial and non-financial). The goals of an organization can be many and varied. They may include operational goals, marketing goals, sales goals, personnel goals, social goals, etc. On the broader scope, goals are usually profit oriented. However, depending upon the state of your industry and the current economic cycle, you might have other objectives, such as conservation of capital, limitations on risk, liquidity, stability of operations over the years, investment programs, future liquidations, or sale of the company.

Once established, these primary goals can then be broken down into sub-goals. For instance, suppose the enterprise has decided to increase its liquidity. Then the accounting department (to choose one example) can determine its sub-goals in terms of accounting, collections, payments and budgeting. The firm could define goals in terms of current ratio, working capital ratios, or labor to sales rations. Similarly, the marketing department could establish new pricing goals, stop pricing based on competitors pricing (who doesn't make money either), stop underpricing because of not knowing cost of sales, or quit offering too many products.

The production department might establish goals to control overhead costs, check invoice pricing versus salesmen's quotes, control waste, or control the material mix within its product. They could better react to external influences such as suppliers, availability of items and economic conditions, and be aware of unusual or unanticipated costs. Finally, they can watch the supply of inventory and expenditures for capital items.

Management must determine adequate staffing levels and retain adequate resources for dividends, bonuses, and salaries. To achieve the organizational goals, these divisional sub-goals must permeate and be coordinated throughout the whole enterprise.

Creating a Simple Spreadsheet

1

Where Do I Start?

As we move forward in our journey of creating projections, it's apparent that everyone has different skill levels and abilities. So where do we start? We start at the very beginning; the basic skills. Some of what we cover may be redundant, but I've always found that there are always basic concepts to learn. I constantly review my basic books and am always amazed to discover new ways of making programming even easier. These solutions have always been in front of me, but it wasn't until further review of basic concepts that I discovered them.

To create a simple spreadsheet in Microsoft® Excel, you enter text, numbers, and formulas. And that is what this chapter is about—the basics!

Parts of an Excel Spreadsheet

1. *Active cell* is the cell with the bold black outline.
2. *Formula bar.* Located above the work area (the cells) of the worksheet. It displays the contents of the active cell. It can also be used for entering or editing data and formulas.
3. *Name box.* Displays the active cell's address or the name of a cell. You can also enter a cell's (or range of cells) name.
4. The columns are named by letters
5. The rows are named by numbers.
6. The tabs at the bottom of a worksheet tell you the worksheet's name.
7. Tools are also grouped by tabs at the top of the worksheet (e.g., **File, Home, Insert**).

8. Within a tab are commands grouped by function (e.g., Clipboard).

9. On the ribbon there are the actual working commands such as **Cut, Copy,** and **Paste.**

10. The Quick Access Toolbar contains shortcuts to common tasks such as: Print, Copy, Paste, Save, etc. They are on the **File** tab➔Quick Access Toolbar.

Entering Data

A cell is a unit in which you enter text, numbers, and formulas. Cells are addressed by their column and row numbers like A1, A2, B1, or B2. You enter data in Excel simply by clicking on a cell and typing within it. Once you click in a cell, it becomes the active cell (fig 1.1). When you finish entering data in a cell, press **Enter** or one of the arrow keys to move to the next cell.

Figure 1.1 The parts of an Excel spreadsheet.

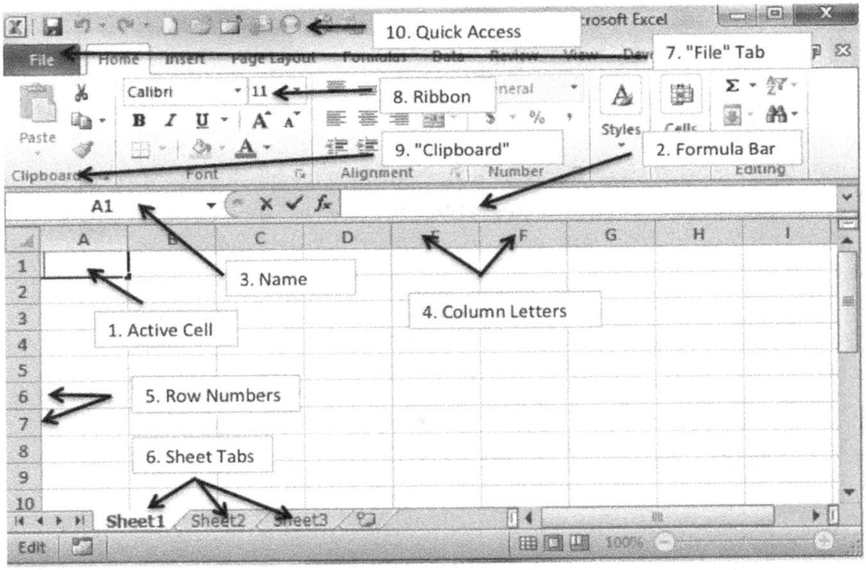

Entering Data Automatically

Instead of entering data one cell at a time, you can use the Autofill feature to fill cells with data based on information in other cells or data that follows a pattern. Use the *fill handle* to enter data automatically. For example, if your data starts with "Jan," you can drag your cursor from the lower left hand corner of that cell and a plus sign (+) will appear (fig 1.2).

Figure 1.2 Using the fill handle

	A	B	C	D
1				
2	Sample Company			
3			Jan	Feb
4	Sales in Units:		10	
5	Average Price Per Unit:		250,000	
6				

Drag your cursor over the adjacent cells you want to automatically fill. Because this group includes patterned data, Excel will automatically fill in the following months. You can also do this with quarters (i.e., Q1, Q2, etc.) and numbers. However, with numbers you need to fill at least two cells (i.e., 1 in A1, 2 in A2) before you can Autofill the subsequent numbers.

Selecting Data

A range is a group of cells in a worksheet that have been selected or highlighted. When cells have been selected, they are surrounded by an outline or border. You can also select ranges, rows, columns, and collections. To select a range, **click and drag** over the desired block of cells (fig 1.3).

Figure 1.3 Click and drag from A2 to C5.

	A	B	C	D
1				
2	Sample Company			
3			Jan	
4	Sales in Units:		10	
5	Average Price Per Unit:		250,000	
6				

Once you have selected a range of cells, you can drag the border to move the selection, or drag the corner of the border to expand it.

In figure 1.3, cells A2 through C5 are selected. These are the cell references of the cells in the upper left and lower right corners of the range. We refer to this range as A2:C5. The two reference points are separated by a colon, which tells Excel to include all the cells between these start and end points.

To select a row, click the row number (fig 1.4).

Figure 1.4 Click on the row number to select an entire row.

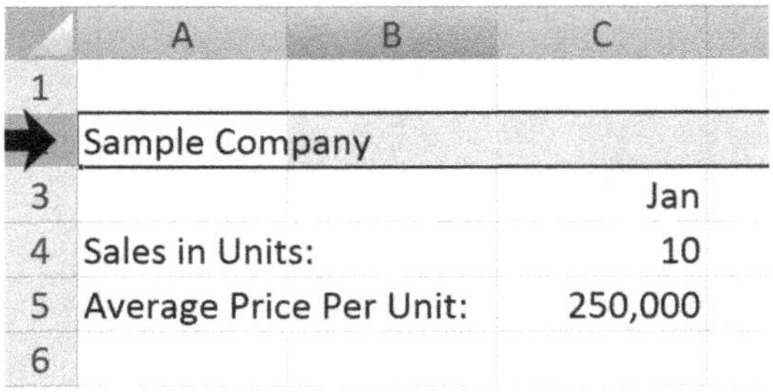

	A	B	C
1			
➡	Sample Company		
3			Jan
4	Sales in Units:		10
5	Average Price Per Unit:		250,000
6			

To select a column, click the column letter, indicated by the arrow (fig 1.5).

Figure 1.5 Click on the column letter to select the entire column.

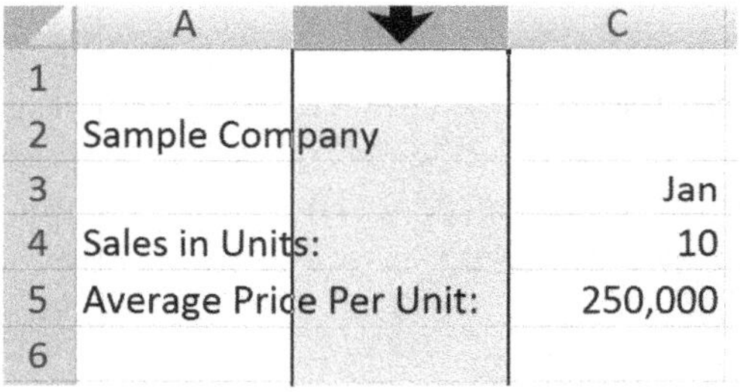

	A	⬇	C
1			
2	Sample Company		
3			Jan
4	Sales in Units:		10
5	Average Price Per Unit:		250,000
6			

To select a collection, hold the **Ctrl** key while you select the rows, columns, and ranges you want. Non-adjacent cell ranges are identified by separating the range of each cell block with commas like A2:B4, or D6:E8. The two cell blocks in the range are A2:B4 and D6:E8.

Finally, to select all the cells in a worksheet, click the **Select All** button, which is at the intersection of the row and column headers (fig 1.6).

Figure 1.6 Select All button

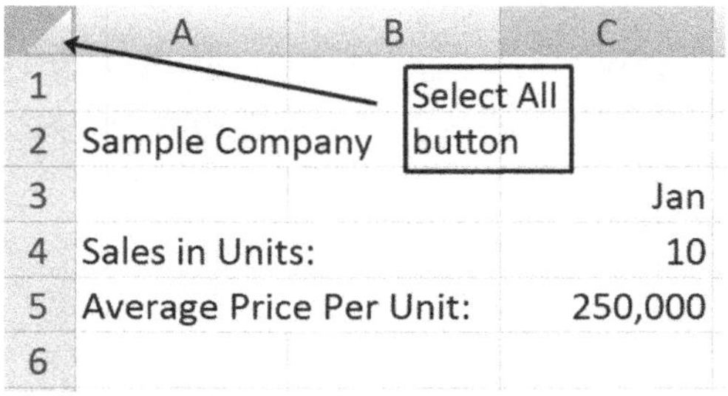

	A	B	C
1		Select All	
2	Sample Company	button	
3			Jan
4	Sales in Units:		10
5	Average Price Per Unit:		250,000
6			

How to Select All Cells in a Blank Worksheet:

- Open a blank Excel worksheet
- Press and hold down the **Ctrl** key on the keyboard
- Press and release the letter A without releasing the **Ctrl** key
- All cells in the worksheet should be selected.

Beware: If there is data on the worksheet, **Ctrl + A** may pick up *only* the immediate adjacent cells, so I do not recommend this method.

Editing Data

To modify data, **double click** the cell you want to change and edit the data that's there. When you finish making your changes, press **Enter.** To cancel the change before you press **Enter,** press **ESC.** You can also edit data by selecting a cell and clicking the contents in the edit line (fig 1.7). To undo your changes, choose Edit-Undo from the Quick Access Toolbar.

Figure 1.7 The arrows show the two ways to edit a cell.

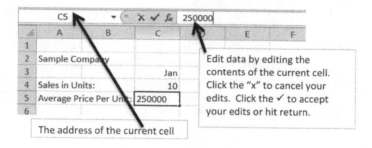

Copying or Moving Data

Using the **Cut, Copy,** and **Paste** commands, you can move or copy entire cells and their contents. You can also copy specific contents or attributes from the cells. For example, you can copy the resulting value of a formula without copying the formula itself, or you can copy only the formula.

- To move cells, click the **Cut** icon (scissors) on the standard toolbar, or press **Ctrl + X.**

- To copy cells, click **Copy** icon (two pages) on the standard toolbar, or press **Ctrl + C.**

- To insert copied information, click **Paste** icon (clipboard and a page) on the standard toolbar, or press **Ctrl + V.**

There is another way to move cells with only your mouse. Select the cell or range you want to move. Move the cursor to the edge of the cell until the cursor changes to a four-pointed arrow. Press the left mouse button, and drag the cell to the new location.

Formatting Cells

You can easily change the format of your data by using the quick format keys (fig 1.8).

Figure 1.8 Change the format of the data in a cell by clicking on the circled section.

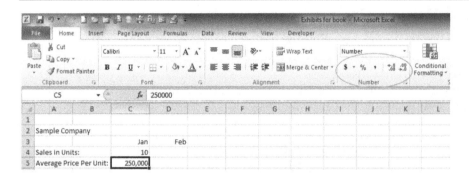

You can also click in a cell and right click. Click on Format Cells from the pop-up menu. This brings up complete Format Cells dialog box.

You can format numbers (using percent, comma, date, currency formatting, etc.), align the text in a cell, change the font, choose colors of both the text and the background, create borders, and protect cells.

Resizing Columns and Rows

You can also adjust the column width and row height. To adjust the column to fit the widest entry, **double click** the border to the right of the column letter. (When you get to the border, a double horizontal arrow with a line through it appears.) To resize to a specific width, drag the border to the right to widen the column or to the left to make it narrower. Excel displays an indicator to show the number of characters the column will hold.

To change the height of a row, drag the bottom border down to make the row taller or drag it up to make it shorter. To adjust the row height to the tallest entry, **double click** the border below the row number. The second way to resize a row or column is to click on the column heading or the row number and then right click. This will bring up the appropriate menu (fig 1.9). With this menu, you can reformat any column or row you wish.

Figure 1.9 Column or Row Menus

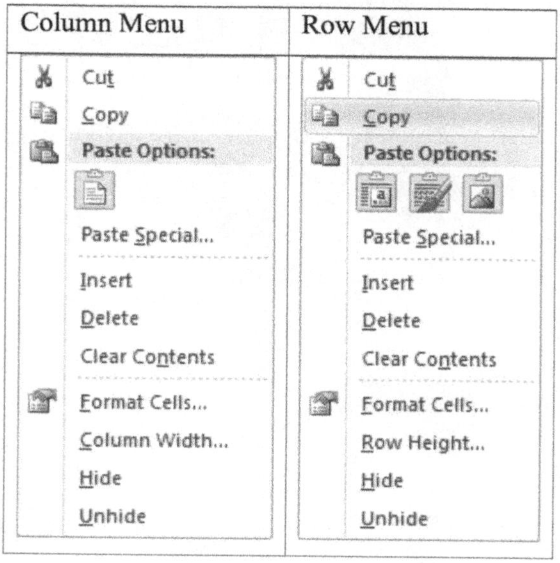

Column Menu	Row Menu
Cut	Cut
Copy	Copy
Paste Options:	Paste Options:
Paste Special...	Paste Special...
Insert	Insert
Delete	Delete
Clear Contents	Clear Contents
Format Cells...	Format Cells...
Column Width...	Row Height...
Hide	Hide
Unhide	Unhide

Calculating Tool

The Autosum feature adds all the data in a group of cells in a single step. Caution: Do not assume that the range the AutoSum selects is always correct. In fact, it is suggested that you NEVER use this feature.

To use the **AutoSum** button:

■ Select the cell where you want the answer to appear;

■ Click the **AutoSum** button located on the **Home** tab in the Editing group. The function will automatically select the closest range of data cells. The selected cells are surrounded by a flashing border (fig 1.10).

■ Make sure you have selected the correct range of cells.

■ If it is correct, press **Enter**.

Figure 1.10 Using the AutoSum button

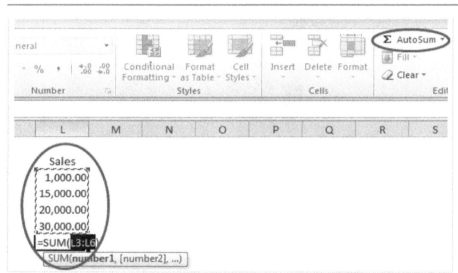

In figure 1.10, the **AutoSum** button is circled in the upper right corner of the **Home** tab. The second circle is a screenshot of what happens when your cursor is in the cell where you want the sum and the **AutoSum** button is clicked.

The AutoSum function has a priority for suggesting a range to include. First, it looks to an uninterrupted group of cells containing data above the active cell. Then it looks for an uninterrupted group of cells containing data to the left of the active cell. If there are no cells adjacent to the active cell, it will put a null formula in – "SUM()" waiting for parameters.

Freezing Panes

You can freeze rows and columns to keep your headings in view while you scroll through the data. When you freeze rows or columns, the frozen cells stay in view even when you scroll through the sheet.

To keep both the first four rows and the first column in figure 1.11 visible, you would click in cell B5. Then go to the **View** tab, click freeze panes, and select Freeze Panes.

Figure 1.11 Freeze Panes

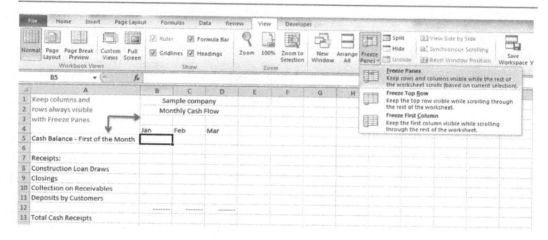

To unfreeze columns, select the freeze panes again and then click Unfreeze Panes (fig 1.12).

Figure 1.12 Unfreeze Panes

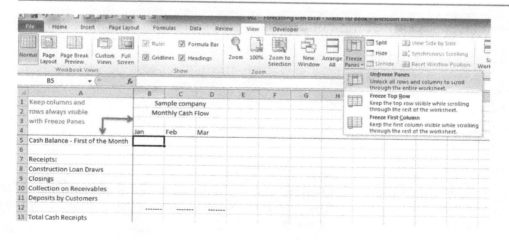

Annotating Cell Contents

Use cell comments to document individual cells of your spreadsheet without taking up valuable display space. Select the cell and **right click**. A pop-up menu will appear. Click on Insert Comment (fig 1.13).

Figure 1.13 Pop-up menu to insert a comment

You will see a box appear with the selected cell. Enter the text that you wish to include as a comment. In this case, we are using cell B2 (fig 1.14).

Figure 1.14 Inserting comments

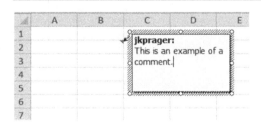

When a cell has a comment, you will see a red comment marker in the top right corner. If you want to edit the comment, **right click** the cell containing the comment, and click Edit Comment.

Naming and Adding Sheets

By default, each workbook in Excel contains three pages or worksheets—*Sheet1*, *Sheet2*, and *Sheet3*. Switching between worksheets is done by clicking on the sheet tab at the bottom of the screen. You can give your worksheet a more appropriate name in order to make your workbook more readable, to help document the contents of the sheet, and to make it easier to find if you have several sheets in your workbook. To change the name of the tab, **double click** on the sheet and type the name you want, or **right click** on the sheet tab to choose Rename (fig 1.15).

Figure 1.15 Bold title indicates the active sheet

You can easily add sheets, name sheets, and customize the way the sheets look in your workbook. To insert a new worksheet at the end of the existing worksheets, click the **Insert Worksheet** tab at the bottom of the screen (fig 1.16).

Figure 1.16 Insert Worksheet tab

You can also **right click** the sheet tab after the one you want to insert click insert and select worksheet. A new worksheet tab will appear before the tab you right clicked.

You can easily change the look of your sheets. For example, you can:

■ Change the default colors in the cells.

■ Add lines around a selected cell by adding a border.

■ Turn off the grid display.

■ Change the default font and colors used for data.

■ Automatically display negative values in red.

That's a review of the basic layout and frequently used commands in building meaningful spreadsheets. Likely, you already knew much of what we just covered, but there were probably one or two points that you had either forgotten or had never used before. The more these foundational elements become second nature to you, the better you'll be able to build on them as we move forward.

The fact is that we've barely scratched the surface—there's plenty more to learn as we move into the next chapter.

More Power with Functions and Formulas

Learning Microsoft® Excel is really about learning to write your own formulas and using Excel functions to save a lot of programming time. Functions are the real value of Excel. Used properly, they will allow you to create spreadsheets in record time. But functions and formulas will fall short if you don't know the difference between absolute and relative referencing.

Think of using formulas like addressing a letter. You can send something to 1 Main Street, but without a city and state or a zip code, the mail may never get to the intended recipient. So, like "1 Main Street", cell A1 could be on *Sheet1*, *Sheet2*, or *Sheet3*. It could even be in an entirely different workbook. Getting in good habits right from the beginning will help you avoid many problems that may evolve in the future.

Writing Your Own Formulas

You can write your own formulas when you need a specialized calculation not found in the functions list. When you press **Enter**, Excel calculates the formula and puts the result in the cell.

Formulas use these standard symbols for operators:

* (asterisk) for multiplication
+ (plus sign) for addition
- (hyphen) for subtraction
/ (forward slash) for division
^ (caret) for exponentiation (e.g., 3^2)

You can create a simple formula to add, subtract, multiply, or divide values in your worksheet. Simple formulas always start with an equal sign (=), followed by constants that are numeric values and calculation operators such as plus (**+**), minus (**-**), asterisk (*****), or forward slash (**/**) signs.

For example, enter the formula: **=5+2*5** in cell C1. Excel multiplies the last two numbers and adds the first number to the result. Following the standard order of mathematical operations, multiplication is performed before addition.

■ On the worksheet, click the cell in which you want to enter the formula.

■ Type the equal sign followed by the constants and operators that you want to use in the calculation.

■ You can enter as many constants and operators in a formula as you need—up to 8,192 characters.

Use Cell References in a Formula

While the formula in the previous step works, it has one drawback. If you want to change the data being calculated you need to edit or rewrite the formula. A better way would be to write formulas so that you can change the data without having to change the formulas themselves. *This is the key to everything else in this book.*

To do this, you need to tell Excel what cells contain the data. A cell's location in the spreadsheet is referred to as its cell reference. To find a cell reference, simply look at the column headings to find which column the cell is in and across to find which row it is in.

The cell reference is a combination of the column letter and row number, such as A1 or B3. Think Apples, Apples, Apples! When writing cell references, the column letter always comes first.

Instead of writing this formula in cell C1: = 5 + 2*5. Put a value of 5 in cell A1 and a value of 2 in cell B1. Then enter this instead: = **A1+B1*A1**. You can refer to a single cell, a range of cells, a location in another worksheet, or a location in another workbook (fig 2.1).

Figure 2.1 Entering a formula

■ As you enter the formula, the first cell reference is A1, the color is blue, and the cell range has a blue border with square corners.

■ The second cell reference is B1, the color is green, and the cell range has a green border with square corners.

■ Note the second reference to A1 is also in blue. If the third reference were to a different cell, it would be in purple and so on.

■ Finally, once you put in the equal sign, you can click on cells, and Excel will type in the reference for you.

Copying Formulas and Functions

Once you put a function or formula in one cell, you can easily copy it to other cells to perform the same calculation on those cells. Select the cell with the formula, choose **Copy** and then highlight the desired cells, and choose **Paste**. Excel copies the formula for each row.

Note: You can also copy formulas into adjacent cells by using the **fill handle**. After verifying that the cell references in the formula are working, select the cell that contains the formula to be copied, and then drag the **fill handle** over the range that you want to fill.

Absolute versus Relative References

In working with spreadsheets, you need to know about relative versus absolute cell references. Absolute and relative references influence the way you copy formulas from one cell to the next.

Relative References

When you copy and paste a formula that contains cell references, what happens to them? If the formula includes relative references, they will change so that the formula is valid and works in its new location. Let's use a simple example. In figure 2.2, we want to multiply the value in cell A1 by the value in cell A2. In cell A3, enter the formula: **=A1*A2**.

Figure 2.2 Using relative cell references

	A	B
1	10	25
2	20	4
3	=A1*A2	=B1*B2

Now **Copy** that formula to cell B3. What happens? The cell references in the formula change when you move them and they work in their new location! This is called a *relative cell reference*. This is the most widely used type of cell reference in formulas.

Absolute References

While relative references change when they are copied, *absolute cell references* always remain the same. To make a cell reference absolute, place a "$" before the column letter or row number that you want to stay the same. For example, "$C$3" refers to cell C3, and will always refer to cell C3, even when you copy the formula to a new location.

TIP: When entering formulas you can use the F4 key after entering a cell reference to toggle among the different relative/absolute versions of that cell address.

In the example in figure 2.3, we have a set commission rate of 10% in cell B2. We want to multiply that by each salesperson's sales. Multiply the rate in cell B2 by the sales in B5, C5, and D5 respectively. In cell B6, we enter the formula: =$B$2*B5. Now, we'll copy that formula over to C6 and D6. Note the B2 doesn't change as we copy it over because we put the "$" before the B and the 2.

Figure 2.3 Using absolute cell references

	INDEX	▼	✕ ✔ *fₓ*	=$B$2*D5	
	A		B	C	D
1					
2	Commission Rate		10%		
3					
4	Salesman		A	B	C
5	Sales		25,000	30,000	20,000
6	Commission		=$B$2*B5	=$B$2*C5	=$B$2*D5

The trick to creating spreadsheets is deciding before you copy a formula which cell references should be relative and which should be absolute. If some cell references refer to input cells in the spreadsheet, you usually want those cells to be absolute.

Figure 2.4 is a summary of using absolute reference. You'll see more of this as we begin to set up our projection.

Figure 2.4 Guide to absolute referencing

$A1	Allows the row reference to change, but not the column reference. This is used when you have a column of constants to reference across columns of cells.
A$1	Allows the column reference to change, but not the row reference. This is used when you have a row of constants to reference across rows of cells.
$A$1	Allows neither the column nor the row reference to change. This is when you have an absolute constant.

You should always set up your worksheets so that you have maximum flexibility to make changes. Do not *hard code* values in a formula. Rather, store the values in separate cells, and use cell references in the formula. Hard code refers to the use of actual values, or constants, in a formula. Using cell references has two advantages:

■ It makes it perfectly clear what values are begin used; they aren't buried in the formula;

■ It makes it easier to change the value.

This may not seem like much of an issue when only one formula is involved, but as you'll see in this book, imagine what will happen if this value were hard coded into several hundred formulas scattered throughout a workbook.

Naming Cells and Ranges

The Name box is the box at the left end of the Formula bar that identifies the selected cell, chart item, or drawing object. The Name box displays the cell reference of the active cell (fig 2.5).

Figure 2.5 The Name box is indicated by the arrow

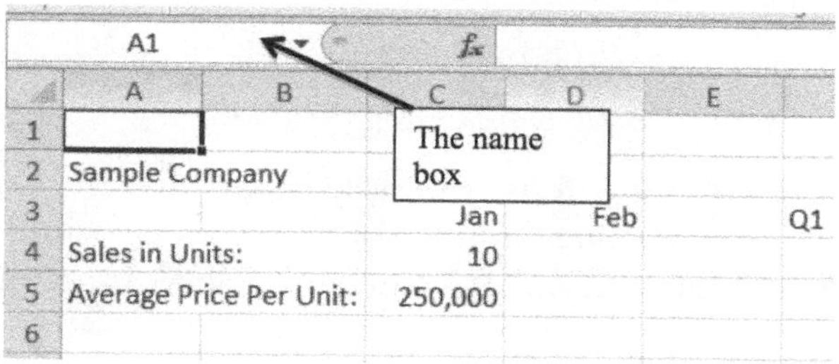

The Name box can also be used to assign names to a cell or range of cells. To do so, select the cell or range you would like to name. Click in the Name box, type the name and press **Enter**. The name appears in the Name box. In figure 2.6, we highlighted cells C3:D3 and named them "Months."

Figure 2.6 The range of highlighted cells is now named Months.

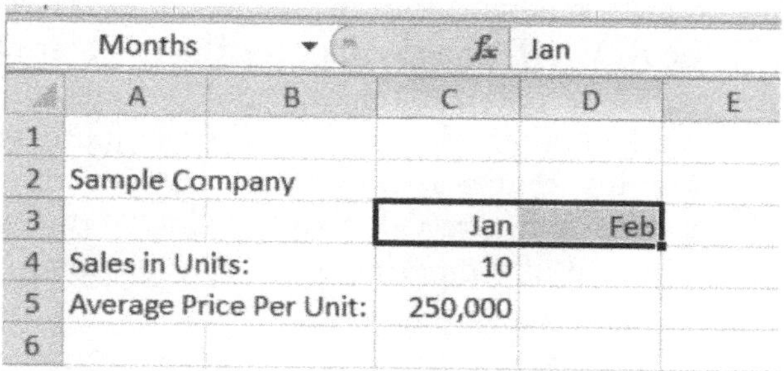

To get to the named range, hit **F5**. A pop-up screen (called an input box) will appear with a list of all the named ranges. Click on the named range you want, and your cursor will go to that range (fig 2.7).

Figure 2.7 The Go To dialog box showing the list of all named ranges

Functions

Excel has built-in formulas called functions that perform many different types of calculations. You can use these functions or write your own formulas to manipulate the data in your spreadsheet.

Using Functions

A function is a prewritten formula that can use multiple inputs or values, perform an operation, and return a value (only one value). You can create formulas using functions. For example, the formula: **=SUM(A1:A2)** uses the SUM function to add the values in cells A1 and A2.

PMT Function

The PMT function calculates the payment on a loan based on constant payments and a constant interest rate. The syntax of an Excel function refers to the layout and order of the function and its arguments. A function's arguments refer to all the data or information required by a function. These arguments must be entered in the correct order.

All functions in Excel begin with the equal sign (=) followed by the function's name, such as *SUM, COUNT,* or *ROUND.* The syntax for the calculating a payment for a loan is as follows: **=PMT(rate, Nper, Pv, Fv, type)**. Rate is the interest rate for the loan; Nper is the total number of payments for the loan; and Pv is the present value, or the total amount that a series of future payments is worth now—also known as the principal. Fv is future value and type is an optional field with "0" if payments are due at the end of the period and "1" if payments are due at the beginning of the period (the default is "0") but for this example we will not be using these arguments.

Suppose we borrow $5,000 to buy a car. We will pay the loan over 36 months with a 5% interest rate—or a monthly rate of 5% divided by 12. We could write a simple formula: **=-PMT(5/12,36,5000)**, to calculate the monthly payment, which comes to $161.34 per month. Note two things about the formula: First, it begins with a minus sign "-". The value this function returns is normally negative, so in order to make the answer a positive number, we put a negative sign in front of the function. Second, there are no spaces between the commas.

When you create a simple formula or a formula that uses a function, you can put the data directly into the formula or refer to data in worksheet cells by including cell references in the formula arguments. In figure 2.8, when you select cell B1, the formula uses the value of that cell to calculate the result. You can also reference a range of cells. The formula shown in cell B5 uses the value in cells B1, B2, and B3 to calculate the payment amount.

Figure 2.8 The PMT function

▲	A	B	C
1	Interest rate	10%	
2	Number of periods	36	
3	Amount of loan	$5,000	
4			
5	Payment	=-PMT(B1/12,B2,B3)	

Again, this formula and function will provide the same results—a payment of $161.34 per month. I could have made each reference an absolute reference as well by putting "$" in front of each column and row reference.

To see all the functions available in Excel, go to the **Formula** tab, click on Insert Function (upper left-hand side), and then a pop-up menu will be displayed (fig 2.9). The Insert Function menu comes with a few commonly used functions. Choose "List All" from the functions menu to select from the full list.

Figure 2.9 Insert Function dialog box

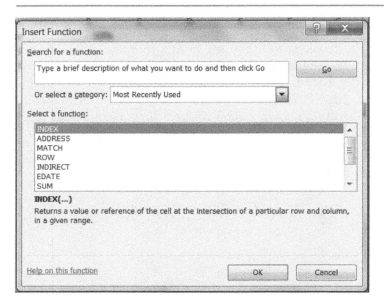

When you select a function, a dialog box like the one shown in figure 2.10 will pop up.

Figure 2.10 Function Arguments dialog box

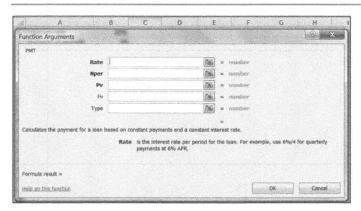

Referring to Another Worksheet in a Formula

For a formula that needs to reference a cell in a different worksheet in the same workbook, use the following format: **=SheetName!CellAddress**. For this example, on *Sheet1* the description "commission rate" is in cell A2 and 10% in cell B2. *Sheet2* is shown in figure 2.11. In cell B4, we want to multiply sales by the commission rate from *Sheet1*, cell B2. The formula would be: **= B3*Sheet1!B2**.

Figure 2.11 Information from *Sheet1* is used in the formula on *Sheet2*.

B4		f_x	=B3*Sheet1!B2	
	A	B	C	D
1				
2				
3	Sales	10,000		
4	Commission	1,000		

To copy that formula to C and D, we would change the formula to: **=B3*Sheet1!$B$2** making *Sheet1*, cell B2 an absolute reference. It doesn't change as you copy the formula to other cells (fig 2.12).

Figure 2.12 The formula in cell D4 is shown in the formula bar.

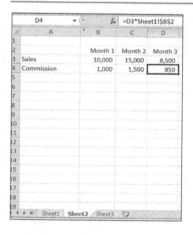

TIP: For worksheet names that include one or more spaces, you will need to enclose it in single quotation marks. The following is a formula that refers to a cell on a sheet by the name of Monthly Sales: =B4*'Monthly Sales'!A12

The Key to Proficiency with Formulas and Functions

We've just scratched the surface of how using formulas and functions is the key to unlocking the real power of Excel. If this seems overwhelming, that's only because these terms and the actions they represent might be new and unfamiliar. I assure you, practice brings a familiarity and comfort with building and using your own formulas.

Remember: The very best golfer, batter, or free-throw shooter at one time had to take his first swing or throw. Developing skills takes practice, practice . . . and more practice. Of course, most of us never reach the level of playing a sport professionally. Still, we may be comfortable playing on a lower level—enjoying an occasional game of golf or a weekend football game with friends. Those skills, while not professional, are enough to allow us to perform comfortably and enjoy the game.

Developing your Excel skills is similar. You don't have to be a professional get value from Excel's formulas and functions. But, like the athlete, the more you practice, the more natural these actions will become. You'll become comfortable experimenting with new formulas and functions, and you'll find that you will get excited at what your numbers can reveal.

Format of a Cash Flow Forecast

3

Cash flow forecasts are used to help determine the impact of cash receipts and expenditures on a company. The basic aim of a forecast is simple—to predict when and in what quantity receipts of cash will come into the company and when and in what quantity payments of cash will be made.

All anticipated receipts of cash are taken into the cash forecast regardless of whether or not they represent income in the accounting sense. Disbursements include payments to subcontractors, suppliers, overhead, etc. Consider your expenses based on past experiences updated for inflation and other various factors. Put your subs on a regular payment schedule, if possible. To help you better estimate purchases, consider creating a budget for each type of job (e.g., model).

Formatting Your Cash Flow Forecast

The basic format of a cash flow statement (fig 3.1) lists current cash balances plus projected receipts (not income) from all sources from which expenses are deducted. Estimating the cash requirements for each job is made easier if you use a standard format.

Figure 3.1 Cash flow forecast standard format

	A	B	C	D	N	O
1		Sample Company				
2		Cash Flow Forecast				
3						
4	Period	1	2	3		
6	Month	Jun-14	Jul-14	Aug-14		Total
8	Sales in Units					12
9						
10	Cash Balance - First of the Month	0	767,000	674,600		0
11						
12	Receipts:					
13	Construction Loan Draws	0	33,750	135,000		2,160,000
14	Closings	0	0	0		3,600,000
15	Collection on Receivables	0	0	0		0
16	Deposits by Customers	0	0	0		0
17		--------	--------	--------		--------
18	Total Cash Receipts	0	33,750	135,000		5,760,000
19						
20	Disbursements					
21	Land Deposit	0	0	60,000		60,000
22	Purchases	0	78,750	225,000		2,700,000
23	Indirect Construction Costs	7,500	7,500	7,500		90,000
24	Financing Costs (Interest)	13,500	13,500	13,500		162,000
25	Marketing Costs	0	14,400	14,400		144,000
26	General & Administrative Costs	12,000	12,000	12,000		144,000
27	Construction Loan Repayments	0	0	0		2,160,000
28		--------	--------	--------		--------
29	Total Disbursements	33,000	126,150	332,400		5,460,000
30		--------	--------	--------		--------
31	Net cash flow for month	-33,000	-92,400	-197,400		300,000
32		--------	--------	--------		--------
33	Cash Excess (Shortage)	-33,000	674,600	477,200		300,000
34	Funds Needed	800,000	0	0		800,000
35	Cash Distributions	0	0	0		-1,100,000
36		--------	--------	--------		--------
37	Cash Balance - End of Month	767,000	674,600	477,200		0
38						

Setting Up the Worksheets

Now that we have reviewed the basics and discussed some of the formulas and functions in Excel, let's create the projection skeleton that will be the foundation for the financial documents we will be working with throughout this book. Go to www.nahb.org/financialforecasting and open the Chapter 3_Projection Skeleton workbook. You will see the *Assumptions* and *Projection* sheets. The skeleton of the cash flow statement is already on the *Projection* sheet. In this chapter we will take you step-by-step through creating your own from scratch.

Let's set up the columns on the *Projection* sheet. **Right click** on column A and a pop-up menu will appear. Select column width, type in *30*, and hit **OK**. The column width is now wider. The width of cells is displayed in characters and pixels rather than in inches (however, 1 inch = 72 characters). When you drag the boundary of a column heading to adjust the width of a column on the worksheet, a ScreenTip displays the width in characters and shows pixels in parentheses.

The height of cells is displayed in points and pixels rather than in inches. When you drag the boundary of a row heading to adjust the height of a row on the worksheet, a ScreenTip displays the height in points and shows pixels in parentheses.

An approximate conversion of points and pixels to inches is shown in table 3.1.

Table 3.1 Conversion chart of points and pixels to inches

Points	Pixels	Inches
18	24	0.25
36	38	0.50
72	96	1.00
108	144	1.50
144	192	2.00

Type the following row descriptions in column A (fig 3.2).

Figure 3.2 List of descriptions for column A of the *Projection* sheet

Next, go to the *Assumptions* sheet to create the chart of assumptions. Make column A 40 characters wide. The title is 18 points and the heading field is colored blue. On the **Home** tab in the font section, select "fill color." Choose a color for your background. Center the title *Project Assumptions* across the columns. Select cells A1:B1➔**right click** and a pop-up menu will appear. Select the **Alignment** tab and in the horizontal category select Center Across Selection. You can put a box around the heading by selecting cells A1:B1, and in the Font box, click on the Outside Borders icon, and select the Outside Borders option (fig 3.3). The circles show the font size, outside borders, and fill color options on the tool bar.

Figure 3.3 Formatting options on the tool bar

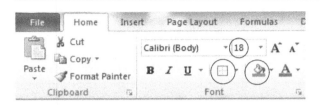

Now add your project parameters to column A on the *Assumptions* sheet (fig 3.4).

Figure 3.4 Project Assumptions in column A on the *Assumptions* sheet

	A	B
1	**Sample Company**	
2		
3	**Project Assumptions**	
4	Project Name	12 Units
5	Beginning Date	Jun-14
6	Length of Proforma (in Months)	12
7	Number of units	12
8	Average Selling Price	300,000
9	Average Cost Per Unit	225,000

EOMONTH and DATE Functions

Now, let's start filling out the columns on the *Projection* sheet.

- For Period: In cell B4, enter the number 1. In cell C4 enter the formula: **=B4+1**

- For Remaining Period: In cell B5, we need the following formula: **=Assumptions! $B$6**. To do that, type an equal sign in cell B5 on the *Projection* sheet. Select the *Assumptions* sheet, and click on cell B6 and press **Enter**. If you want to make this an absolute reference, then hit **F2** (the edit key) and then put a "$" before the B and the 5 or hit **F4** and excel will do it for you. Note: Excel puts in the page reference "Assumptions!"

- In cell C5 on the *Projection* sheet, enter the formula: **=B5-1**.

- In cell B6 type an equal sign. Select the *Assumptions* sheet, and click on cell B5. Format this cell by **right clicking** in the cell. Select the date on the Format Cells dialog box then select the format May 01.

- In the cell C6, we have a choice of entries:

- **=EOMONTH(B6,1)** Use the EOMONTH function when you want to get the last day of the month in future or past months. The syntax is as follows: **=EOMONTH(start_date, months)**. Where the second argument (months) is the number of months after a start date. In our case, we want the next month.

- We could also use this formula to add a month: **=DATE(YEAR (B6),MONTH(B6)+1,DAY(A1))** With the DATE function, the arguments are always in the following order (year, month, day)—whatever the date format specified in your regional parameters. Suppose you want to pick the middle of the month for each following month. Your formula would be: **=DATE(YEAR(B6),MONTH(B6)+1,15)**.

- Format the cell by **right clicking** on the cell, select the Format Cells dialog box, and then select Date and the format May-01.

- The date functions are strictly a matter of preference.

■ Highlight the range C4:C6, and drag the lower right hand corner to cell M6. Your spreadsheet should look like figure 3.5.

Figure 3.5 The *Projection* sheet after using the EOMONTH and DATE functions

	A	B	C	D	E	F	G	H	I	J	K	L	M	N
1						Sample Company								
2						Cash Flow Statement								
3														
4	Period		1	2	3	4	5	6	7	8	9	10	11	12
5	Remaining Periods		12	11	10	9	8	7	6	5	4	3	2	1
6	Month		Jun-14	Jul-14	Aug-14	Sep-14	Oct-14	Nov-14	Dec-14	Jan-15	Feb-15	Mar-15	Apr-15	May-15	Total

■ In cell N8, type in the formula: **=SUM(B8:M8)**. This formula adds all the values for the 12 months.

■ In cell B10, enter the number 0. In cell C10, enter the formula: **=B36**. The beginning cash for the month is the ending cash of the preceding month. **Copy** the formula over to cell M10. In cell N10, enter the formula: **=B10**. Column N is the total column, and we want to be able to prove our work, so beginning cash at the beginning of the projection is the number that belongs here.

■ In cells B17, B27, B29, B31, B35 enter -------- and right justify that cell. You can also do this by clicking on cell B17 and hitting **Ctrl + C**. This copies the formula in cell B17. Then move the cursor to the appropriate cells and type **Ctrl + V**.

■ In cell B18, enter the formula: **=SUM(B12:B17)**. Note: the formula includes the underlines. This is a trick in Excel that allows you to add lines between B12 and the underline. When you do that, the SUM formula will adjust automatically, saving you a lot of programming time.

- In cell B28, enter the formula: **=SUM(B20:B27)**
- In cell B30, enter the formula: **=B18-B28**
- In cell B32, enter the formula: **=B10+B30**
- In cell B36, enter the formula: **=SUM(B32:B35)**
- Now highlight cells B17:B36, and drag the formulas over to cell N36. Your spreadsheet should look like the one in figure 3.6.

Figure 3.6 The *Projection* sheet after adding all the formulas

	A	B	C	D	E	F	G	H	I	J	K	L	M	N
1						Sample Company								
2						Cash Flow Forecast								
3														
4	Period	1	2	3	4	5	6	7	8	9	10	11	12	
5	Remaining Periods	12	11	10	9	8	7	6	5	4	3	2	1	
6	Month	Jun-14	Jul-14	Aug-14	Sep-14	Oct-14	Nov-14	Dec-14	Jan-15	Feb-15	Mar-15	Apr-15	May-15	Total
7	Sales in Units													
8														
9	Cash Balance - First of the Month	0	0	0	0	0	0	0	0	0	0	0	0	0
10														
11	Receipts:													
12	Construction Loan Draws													0
13	Closings													0
14	Collection on Receivables													0
15	Deposits by Customers													0
16														
17	Total Cash Receipts	0	0	0	0	0	0	0	0	0	0	0	0	0
18														
19	Disbursements													
20	Land Deposit													0
21	Purchases													0
22	Indirect Construction Costs													0
23	Financing Costs (Interest)													0
24	Marketing Costs													0
25	General & Administrative Costs													0
26	Construction Loan Repayments													0
27														
28	Total Disbursements	0	0	0	0	0	0	0	0	0	0	0	0	0
29														
30	Net cash flow for month	0	0	0	0	0	0	0	0	0	0	0	0	0
31														
32	Cash Excess (Shortage)	0	0	0	0	0	0	0	0	0	0	0	0	0
33	Funds Needed													
34	Cash Distributions													
35														
36	Cash Balance - End of Month	0	0	0	0	0	0	0	0	0	0	0	0	0

Now let's add the column totals.

- In cell N6, type the header *Total* and right justify it.
- Highlight cell N8. **Copy** the formula and **Paste** it into the following ranges:
  - N13:N16
  - N21:N26
  - N33:N34
- Highlight cells A1:N2. **Right click** and select Format Cells, click on the **Alignment** tab, and in the horizontal text selection drop-down box select Center Across Selection (fig 3.7).

Figure 3.7 The *Projection* sheet with the column totals included

	A	B	C	D	E	F	G	H	I	J	K	L	M	N
1						Sample Company								
2						Cash Flow Forecast								
3														
4	Period	1	2	3	4	5	6	7	8	9	10	11	12	
5	Remaining Periods	12	11	10	9	8	7	6	5	4	3	2	1	
6	Month	Jun-14	Jul-14	Aug-14	Sep-14	Oct-14	Nov-14	Dec-14	Jan-15	Feb-15	Mar-15	Apr-15	May-15	Total
7	Sales in Units						1	2	2	3	2	1	1	12
8														
9	Cash Balance - First of the Month	0	0	0	0	0	0	0	0	0	0	0	0	0
10														
11	Receipts:													
12	Construction Loan Draws													
13	Closings													0
14	Collection on Receivables													0
15	Deposits by Customers													0
16														
17	Total Cash Receipts	0	0	0	0	0	0	0	0	0	0	0	0	0
18														
19	Disbursements													
20	Land Deposit													
21	Purchases													0
22	Indirect Construction Costs													0
23	Financing Costs (Interest)													0
24	Marketing Costs													0
25	General & Administrative Costs													0
26	Construction Loan Repayments													0
27														
28	Total Disbursements	0	0	0	0	0	0	0	0	0	0	0	0	0
29														
30	Net cash flow for month	0	0	0	0	0	0	0	0	0	0	0	0	0
31														
32	Cash Excess (Shortage)	0	0	0	0	0	0	0	0	0	0	0	0	0
33	Funds Needed													
34	Cash Distributions													
35														
36	Cash Balance - End of Month	0	0	0	0	0	0	0	0	0	0	0	0	0

Inserting Rows and Columns

Now the shell is complete. But, we still have to insert rows. The trick to adding rows is to add the dashes (I use seven ------- dashes) and use that as part of the sum total. Thus, to add a row, we only have to click in a cell, **right click**, select Insert, and pick Entire row or Entire column from the menu (fig 3.8).

Figure 3.8 The Insert drop down box with Entire row selected.

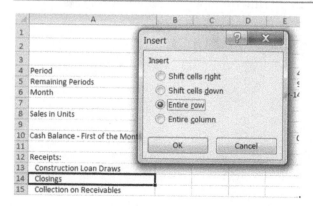

To add a row to a spreadsheet, you can also:

- **Right click** on the row header below where you want the new row added.
- Choose Insert from the menu or **Ctrl +**. (If don't have a plus sign on a number pad, then hit **Shift Ctrl +**.)
- The new row will be inserted above the row you selected.
- To add more than one new row, we select more than one row in the row header.
- In the row header, select the number of rows you want added to the spreadsheet.
- **Right click** on the selected rows.
- Choose Insert from the menu or **Ctrl +**.
- The new rows will be inserted above the rows you first selected.
- These same steps apply for adding both rows and columns.

Now, highlight cell N8, **Copy** the formula and **Paste** it into the following ranges:

- N13:N16
- N21:N26
- N33:N34

In this example, if you insert rows and columns, the SUM formula will adjust automatically *after* the data is put into the inserted cells. Get in the habit of checking your formulas to make sure they are adjusting correctly after you insert and/or delete columns.

The Skeleton

You can save yourself a lot of time and energy by putting together a skeleton and then creating formulas within the skeleton. The key functions of this chapter are: EOMONTH, DATE, and SUM. Experiment with these functions, as they will be used repeatedly. Mastery of these functions will help you progress.

Your Sales Forecast

4

Step 2. Determine Your Cash Inflows from Sales

In the Introduction, we said there are eight steps in creating a forecast. In Step 2, our goal is to calculate sales revenues. This is probably the most critical element in the projection, as this is the first place an investor normally looks within the projection. They will be concerned with your assumptions about absorption and pricing. If not realistic, the credibility of your projection is in jeopardy.

Probably the most critical estimate in cash flow forecasting is determining unit sales. Usually sales represent the principal source of cash receipts. Once you have your estimated sales in units, you can generate the estimated revenues associated with those sales to fill out your sales forecast. And in order to know where you're going, it is helpful to know where you have been.

Your Monthly Sales

If possible, review your sales month-by-month from the last few years. What historical trend emerges from this review? Figure 4.1 shows what a chart of monthly sales might look like.

Figure 4.1 Chart of sales by month

Year	2010	2011	2012	2013	Avg	% of Year
Jan						
Feb						
Mar						
Apr						
May						
Jun						
Jul						
Aug						
Sep						
Oct						
Nov						
Dec						
Total						100%

Monthly Sales

Once you know your historical sales trend, you can create a sales forecast for the current year. You can adjust your sales forecast to take into consideration a market approach or an internal build-up approach. The market approach looks at the market as a whole and determines how much of the market you can capture. The buildup approach calculates the amount of units you are capable of building. Your sales goal normally is the lower of the two approaches. Here's how to do it:

- Market approach:
  - Determine the total units in the market.
  - Estimate your share of the market.
  - Set a sales goal based upon your estimate of your share of the total market.
- Now, look at your internal components to make sure that your sales forecast is achievable (the internal build-up approach):
  - Available lots
  - Production capacity
  - Growth capabilities (organization strength)
  - Market acceptance of the product
  - Local lending climate
  - Sales capacity

Now temper your sales forecasts by considering the following factors and adjust as necessary:

- Past sales volume
- Pricing policies

- General economic and industry conditions
- Advertising and other promotion
- Competitive conditions
- Seasonal variations
- Production capacity

Let's look again at the document we have been working on. The skeleton created in Chapter 3 serves as the foundation for the work that comes next. Go to www.nahb.org/financialforecasting and open the Chapter 4_Your Sales Forecast workbook. Let's start adding some muscle.

Let's assume we are selling 12 units, between November 2014 and May 2015. Fill out the sales in units on line 8 of the *Projection* sheet (fig 4.2).

Figure 4.2 Line 8 shows 12 units sold between November and May.

	A	B	C	D	E	F	G	H	I	J	K	L	M	N
1						Sample Company								
2						Cash Flow Forecast								
3														
4	Period		1	2	3	4	5	6	7	8	9	10	11	12	
5	Month		Jun-14	Jul-14	Aug-14	Sep-14	Oct-14	Nov-14	Dec-14	Jan-15	Feb-15	Mar-15	Apr-15	May-15	Total
6	Year		2014	2014	2014	2014	2014	2014	2014	2015	2015	2015	2015	2015	
7															
8	Sales in Units							1	2	2	3	2	1	1	12

Now we need to calculate the average price per unit for the project. To do so, click on the *Avg Price & Costs* sheet (fig 4.3).

Figure 4.3 Average selling price and average cost per unit

	A	B	C	D
1		Sample Company		
2		12 Units		
3				
4			Selling	Total
5	Unit Description	Units	Price	Revenues
6	Model A	4	250,000	1,000,000
7	Model B	4	300,000	1,200,000
8	Model C	4	350,000	1,400,000
9		--------		--------
10	Total	12		3,600,000
11	Avg.			300,000

On the *Assumptions* sheet, link cell B8 to cell D11 on the *Avg Price & Costs* sheet by using this formula: **=+'Avg Price & Costs'!D11** (fig 4.4). Note: there are spaces in the tab name so its apostrophes are before and after the sheet name.

Figure 4.4 The average selling price calculated on the *Avg Price & Costs* sheet

---

	A	B
3	**Project Assumptions**	
4	Project Name	12 Units
5	Beginning Date	Jun-14
6	Length of Proforma (in Months)	12
7	Number of units	12
8	Average Selling Price	300,000
9	Average Cost Per Unit	

To see all the formulas in your spreadsheet (fig 4.5), press **Ctrl + `** (grave accent in the upper left part of the keyboard).

Figure 4.5 *Avg Price & Costs* sheet with all the formulas shown

---

	A	B	C	D
1	**=+Assumptions!A1**			
2	**=+Assumptions!B4**			
3				
4			Selling	Total
5	Unit Description	Units	Price	Revenues
6	Model A	4	250000	=+B6*C6
7	Model B	4	300000	=+B7*C7
8	Model C	4	350000	=+B8*C8
9		--------		--------
10	Total	=SUM(B6:B9		=SUM(D6:D9)
11	Avg.			=+D10/B10

Note the following:

■ Cells A1 and A2 refer to the *Assumptions* sheet. Thus, you can change the company project name, and the spreadsheet will adjust automatically.

■ Cells A6:A8 are the model names.

■ B6:B8 and C6:C8 are the units and selling prices of the models.

■ D6:D8 represents the number of units to be sold multiplied by the selling prices for each unit to create total revenue by model.

- Line 10 is the total number of units (which will link back to the *Assumptions* page, cell B7) and total revenue.

- Cell D11 is the average price per unit (which links back to the *Assumptions* page). It is total revenues (D10) divided by total number of units (B10).

- I use average prices as the actual model to be sold in any given month as an estimate. No projection will be 100% accurate, but this is like a game of horse-shoes—you just want to be close.

Your Sales Revenues

Yes, we are finally ready to enter in some cash. Click again on the *Projection* sheet.

Go to cell B14 and multiply line B8 (the sales units) by Assumptions!B8 (the average sales price). The formula will look like this: **=B$8*Assumptions!$B$8**. Note the "$" before the Assumptions!$B$8 as a reference in the *Assumptions* sheet. The average price will not change while the sales for the month is relative to the month you are in. (Note: the first B$8 is an absolute reference to the row only, not the column.)

Finally, copy that formula to cells B14:M14. Note that our cash balances are already beginning to show the effect of our calculations (fig 4.6).

Figure 4.6 The sample cash flow statement with the estimated sales figures included

	A	B	C	D	E	F	G	H	I	J	K	L	M	N
1							Sample Company							
2							Cash Flow Forecast							
3														
4	Period	1	2	3	4	5	6	7	8	9	10	11	12	
6	Month	Jun-14	Jul-14	Aug-14	Sep-14	Oct-14	Nov-14	Dec-14	Jan-15	Feb-15	Mar-15	Apr-15	May-15	Total
7	Year	2014	2014	2014	2014	2014	2014	2014	2015	2015	2015	2015	2015	
8	Sales in Units						1	2	2	3	2	1	1	12
9														
10	Cash Balance - First of the Month	0	0	0	0	0	0	300,000	900,000	1,500,000	2,400,000	3,000,000	3,300,000	0
11														
12	Receipts:													
13	Construction Loan Draws													
14	Closings	0	0	0	0	0	300,000	600,000	600,000	900,000	600,000	300,000	300,000	3,600,000

Note the use of absolute and relative references in the formulas, which were discussed in Chapter 2. Take the time to watch how they change under various scenarios. Over time, the liberal use of the "$" sign will save you many hours of debugging.

We exist in business to make sales and/or close units. Without the proper level of sales, we can't exist. But more importantly, the cash flow from sales is a prime consideration in running a business. You can exist without profits, but you can't stay in business one day without cash. It takes money to make money. Now it is time to project our average costs per unit.

Scheduling Your Production Costs

5

Step 3 in our journey is to schedule the costs of production. For most businesses, costs are incurred and paid long before the cash from the sale is received. Take a typical homebuilder. You might be building a home for 90–180 days. During that time you will have to pay your vendors and ensure that you have the cash to do so. How you finance those expenditures is one of the purposes of a projection. Cash can come from sales, loans, and equity (putting money into the company). Planning for cash flow disruptions is your responsibility.

Step 3. Schedule Your Costs of Production

After sales are budgeted, you can prepare the production budget. Go to www.nahb.org/financialforecasting and open the Chapter 5_Production Costs workbook. Click on the *Avg Price & Costs* sheet. In the previous chapter, we calculated average selling price. Now, we will extend that worksheet to include average costs per unit. You will see the cost per unit information has been added (fig 5.1).

- In this step, we will multiply the number of units of each model by their cost per unit

- After determining total costs of each model, we add all the models to determine total costs

- Divide total costs by number of units to determine the average cost per unit.

Figure 5.1 Calculating average production costs

	F	G	H	I
4			Cost Per	Cost
5	Unit Description	Units	Unit	Per/Unit
6	Model A	4	187,500	750,000
7	Model B	4	225,000	900,000
8	Model C	4	262,500	1,050,000
9		--------		--------
10	Total	12		2,700,000
11	Avg.			225,000

On the *Assumptions* sheet, link cell B9 to cell Ill on the *Avg Price & Costs* sheet by using this formula: **=+'Avg Price & Costs'!I11**.

Consider the following when budgeting your production costs:

- Timing of disbursements (how long is your production cycle—e.g., for a home you incur costs for 6 months before you finally sell it)
- Material usage and purchases
- Direct labor costs
- Indirect variable costs

For purposes of cash flow, determine when you will incur costs and receive the draws from your lenders for the jobs. We want to enter the purchases on our cash flow statement as we make them. And we want to enter loan proceeds on our cash flow statement as we receive them.

Suppose we are constructing a home that costs us $225,000, and we can sell it 5 months after we begin construction. It costs us 35% of total costs in the first month of construction, 30% in the second, 25% in the third, and 10% in the fourth month. We sell the unit the month after completion. You will find all this information is now included on the *Assumptions* sheet (fig 5.2).

Figure 5.2 Spreadsheet showing costs throughout the production cycle

	A	B
29	**Purchases/Borrowings**	
30		Purchases
31	Month of Sale	0.0%
32	1 Month before sale	10.0%
33	2 Months before sale	25.0%
34	3 Months before sale	30.0%
35	4 Months before sale	35.0%
36	5 Months before sale	0.0%
37	6 Months before sale	0.0%
38	Total	100.0%

For financial statement purposes, these expenses would be categorized as inventory until the day of sale. But you are out the cash. This is a major reason that we highly prefer a cash flow forecast to a financial forecast. We will create the financial statements later.

TIP: Don't start with financial statements; it is misleading us as to our cash needs.

How can we project our cash needs as accurately as possible? The next section will show you how, and it can get pretty complicated. If you don't want all the detail, take a shortcut and use the formula shown in figure 5.15 on page XX.

Determining the Timing of Purchases

There are three functions that need to be used to do this on one line within the projections: SUMPRODUCT, OFFSET, and MIN. Let's introduce you to the functions first.

SUMPRODUCT Function

The SUMPRODUCT formula multiplies the numbers in one list (array) by the corresponding numbers in a different list. Then it adds the results together to arrive at the total sum. It sums the products, hence the name SUMPRODUCT. The syntax is: **=SUMPRODUCT(list 1, list 2, etc.).**

Let's say you have three products. One sells for $5, another for $10, and the third for $20. During the month, you sell 2 of the first, 3 of the second, and 4 of the more expensive one. What were your revenues?

Using SUMPRODUCT, if you have data like (2,3,4) in one list and (5,10,20) in another list, you will get 120 (because 2*5 + 3*10 + 4*20 is 120). The key to this formula is the order (fig 5.3).

Figure 5.3 Simple example of the SUMPRODUCT function

	A	B	C	D	E	F	G
1		Product A	Product B	Product C			
2	Sales	2	3	4	=SUMPRODUCT(B2:D2,B3:D3)		
3	Price	5	10	20	=2*5+3*10+4*20		
4					=10+30+80 = 120		

Using the parameters from figure 5.2, assume that you have a construction schedule that will take four months, and you close the unit in month five. We know that our average cost of construction is $225,000 per unit. You will spend 35% ($78,750) of those costs four months before closing, 30% ($67,500) of those costs three months before closing, 25% ($56,250) two months before closing, and 10% ($22,500) one month before closing. If you put this in a spreadsheet, our formulas production costs might look like figure 5.4.

Figure 5.4 Calculating production costs with a four month production schedule, selling the unit in month five

	A	B	C	D	E	F	G	H
1	Month		1	2	3	4	5	
2	Months before sale		4	3	2	1	0	
3	Constuction costs		78,750	67,500	56,250	22,500	0	
4	Sales		0	0	0	0	1	
5								
6	Purchases							
7	Month of Sale						0	=$G$2*G$4
8	1 Month Before Sale					22,500		=$F$2*G$4
9	2 Months Before Sale				56,250			=$E$2*G$4
10	3 Months Before Sale			67,500				=$D$2*G$4
11	4 Months Before Sale		78,750					=$C$2*G$4
12			--------	--------	--------	--------	--------	
13	Purchases		78,750	67,500	56,250	22,500	0	

This gets the basic idea, but it only works well if nothing changes. What if you have a sale in month five and month six? What are your costs every month as you build both homes? This spreadsheet is not flexible enough to allow for this. One solution is to work backward from every sale. You can inverse the costs (fig 5.5).

Figure 5.5 Production costs with the costs now inverted

	A	B	C	D	E	F	G
14							
15				Months before closing			
16			0	1	2	3	4
17	Inverse of Costs		0	22,500	56,250	67,500	78,750

Now let's put our sales on line 20 (shaded). Cell C21 (circled) contains the formula: **=SUMPRODUCT($C$17:$G$17,C20:G20)** (fig 5.6).

Figure 5.6 Cell C21 shows the SUMPRODUCT of the production costs from line 17 and the sales from line 20.

	A	B	C	D	E	F	G
15				Months before closing			
16			0	1	2	3	4
17	Inverse of Costs		0	22,500	56,250	67,500	78,750
18							
19	Month		1	2	3	4	5
20	Sales		0	0	0	0	1
21	Production Costs		78,750				

This is similar to the simple product sales per month calculation we did in figure 5.3. In figure 5.6, we have data of {0,0,0,0,1} in one list (sales) and {0,22500,56250,67500,78750} in another list (the inverse of the cost per month). When we apply SUMPRODUCT, you will get $78,750 (because 0*0 + 22500*0 + 56250*0 + 67500*0 + 78750*1 is $78,750).

Let's add a sale in month six as well as one in month five. What happens to our costs each month? Figure 5.7 looks at month one (cell D21) first.

Figure 5.7 Copying the SUMPRODUCT formula from C21 to D21 provides the production costs for month one.

	A	B	C	D	E	F	G	H
15				Months before closing				
16			0	1	2	3	4	
17	Inverse of Costs		0	22,500	56,250	67,500	78,750	
18								
19	Month		1	2	3	4	5	6
20	Sales		0	0	0	0	1	1
21	Production Costs		78,750					
22				=SUMPRODUCT($C$17:$G$17,D20:H20)				

The shaded cells show sales in months five and six. In cell D21 our formula adjusted to being copied from C21. (Note the constants $C$17:$G$17 did not change because these are the costs by month, regardless of when the process begins.) Because we move the sales formula over one cell to the right, C20:G20 becomes D20:H20. These are relative references (current month sales through sales 5 months out). If you apply SUMPRODUCT, you will get $146,250 (because [C17*D20] + [D17*E20] + [E17*F20] + [F17*G20] + [G17*H20] is really 0*0 + 22500*0 + 56250*0 + 67500*1 + 78750*1 = $146,250).

This allows for some variances that the earlier step did not, which is a move in the right direction. We could simply continue to copy the formula over to all the cells, but by doing so something weird can happen. You could start accumulating the costs for the total column or extraneous columns. You need to constrain the formula by lessening the timeframe to build the home or the remaining months in the projection. In order to create reusable templates to create cost projections, we need two more functions: OFFSET and MIN.

OFFSET Function

The OFFSET function allows you to insert rows or columns into a spreadsheet without retyping formulas that reference the row before. It returns a reference *to* a range that is a specified number of rows and columns *from* a cell or range of cells. The reference that is returned can be a single cell or a range of cells. You can specify the number of rows and the number of columns to be returned. The syntax is as follows:

=OFFSET (reference, rows, cols, height, width)

Reference is the original cell from which you want to base the offset. Rows is the number of rows, up or down; they can be positive (below the starting reference) or negative (above the starting reference). Cols is the number of columns (to the left or right) that you want the upper-left cell of the result to reference. Cols can be positive (to the right of the starting reference) or negative (to the left of the starting reference). Height is the height, in number of rows that you want the returned reference to be. Width is the width, in number of columns that you want the returned reference to be. Height and width must both be a positive number. They are also optional arguments—they aren't required for the OFFSET function to work

Example 1: Let the OFFSET be to a single cell. In figure 5.8, the formula in cell B2 is: **=OFFSET(B2,-1,0)**. Following the syntax: B2 is the current column and row, and this command sets B2 equal to the value one row up (-1) and the same column (0) or the value in B1. If you hit **Enter**, the value in B2 would be 10.

Figure 5.8 The OFFSET formula in cell B2 refers back to the value in B1.

PMT		▾	X ✓ *fx*	=OFFSET(B2,-1,0)	
◢	A	B	C	D	E
1		10			
2		=OFFSET(B2,-1,0)			

If you were to insert a row between B1 and B2 as shown in figure 5.9, then the OFFSET would start at B3. Since one cell up (-1) in the same column (0) refers to an empty cell (B2), the value in cell B3 is zero.

Figure 5.9 The same OFFSET formula is now in cell B3.

B3		▼		*fx*	=OFFSET(B3,-1,0)
◢	A	B	C	D	E
1		10			
2					
3		0			

Example 2: Let OFFSET equal a range of rows or columns. The formula is: **=OFFSET(A1,1,1,4,3)** and refers to cell A1 as the starting point. The next two numbers (1,1) tell you to move one row down and one column over. The last two numbers (4,3) define the size of the range you want to return. So, 4,3 would give you a range 4 cells tall and 3 cells wide. In other words, we would get the range B2:D5. We would use this offset in conjunction with another command such as SUM (fig 5.10).

Figure 5.10 Using the OFFSET function to reference a cell range

---

C7		▼		*fx*	=SUM(OFFSET(A1,1,1,3,3))	
◢	A	B	C	D	E	F
1	1	6	11	16		
2	2	7	12	17		
3	3	8	13	18		
4	4	9	14	19		
5	5	10	15	20		
6						
7			117			
8			=SUM(OFFSET(A1,1,1,3,3))			

Suppose we want to multiply one array (list) by another. The first list is in cells B2:B5, and the second is in cells C2:C5. We could use a simple SUMPRODUCT formula in A1: **=-SUMPRODUCT(B2:B5,C2:C5)** or we could use the OFFSET function: **=SUMPRODUCT(OFFSET(A1,1,1,4,1),OFFSET(A1,1,2,4,1))**. This is more work up front, but you'll soon see the usefulness.

In our SUMPRODUCT example from figure 5.7, let's substitute: **=SUM PRODUCT(OFFSET($C$17,0,0,1,5),D20:H20)** for: **=SUMPRODUCT($C$17: $G$17,D20:H20)**. Now our spreadsheet will look like figure 5.11.

Figure 5.11 Using the OFFSET function in cell E24 to add the production costs of a second house

	A	B	C	D	E	F	G	H
14								
15				Months before closing				
16			0	1	2	3	4	
17	Inverse of costs		0	22,500	56,250	67,500	78,750	
18								
19	Month		1	2	3	4	5	6
20	Remaining Periods		6	5	4	3	2	1
21	Sales		0	0	0	0	1	1
22			78,750	146,250	123,750	78,750	22,500	0
23				=SUMPRODUCT($C$17:$G$17,D20:H20)				
24				=SUMPRODUCT(OFFSET($C$17,0,0,1,5),D20:H20)				
25			Total Costs		450,000			
26								

As you can see, it costs \$450,000 (2*\$225,000) to build the two homes, which is the correct answer. But watch what happens when we add a total column (fig 5.12). The formula did not recognize that cell I20 was a total and calculated accumulating costs related to the total column.

Figure 5.12 The OFFSET function

	A	B	C	D	E	F	G	H	I
14									
15				Months before closing					
16			0	1	2	3	4		
17	Inverse of costs		0	22,500	56,250	67,500	78,750		
18									
19	Month		1	2	3	4	5	6	Total
20	Remaining Periods		6	5	4	3	2	1	
21	Sales		0	0	0	0	1	1	2
22			78,750	146,250	123,750	78,750	22,500	0	
23				=SUMPRODUCT($C$17:$G$17,D20:H20)					
24				=SUMPRODUCT(OFFSET($C$17,0,0,1,5),D20:H20)					
25			Total Costs		900,000				

How do we solve this problem? Now for the MIN function.

MIN and MAX Function

The MIN function returns the smallest number in a set of values. The syntax for the MIN function is: **=MIN(number1,number2, etc.)** Arguments can be numbers, named ranges, arrays, or cell references.

As long as we are discussing the MIN function, let's also look at the MAX function, which returns the largest number in a set of values. Its syntax is: **=MAX (number1,number2, etc.)**

We want to use the MIN function to adjust the formula to take the lesser of the construction period or the remaining months. First, add a line called "Remaining

Months", which is done by inserting a line before line 20 and making cell C20 = H19. In cell D20, the formula is: **=C20-1.** and **Copy** that formula from cell D20:H20 (fig 5.13).

Figure 5.13 Using the MIN function in line 20

	A	B	C	D	E	F	G	H
14								
15					Months before closing			
16			0	1	2	3	4	
17	Inverse of costs		0	22,500	56,250	67,500	78,750	
18								
19	Month		1	2	3	4	5	6
20	Remaining Periods		6	5	4	3	2	1

Next we change the SUMPRODUCT formula in cell C22 (formerly C21 before we inserted row 20) as follows:

$$=SUMPRODUCT(OFFSET(\$C\$17,0,0,1,5),OFFSET(C21,0,0,1,5))$$

Finally we substitute MIN($G$16+1,C$20) for the 5, and our formula looks like this:

$$=SUMPRODUCT(OFFSET(\$C\$17,0,0,1,MIN(\$G\$16+1,C\$20)),$$
$$OFFSET(C21,0,0,1,MIN(\$G\$16+1,C\$20)))$$

Our spreadsheet now has the correct total costs of $450,000 (fig 5.14).

Figure 5.14 The SUMPRODUCT, OFFSET, and MIN functions

	A	B	C	D	E	F	G	H	I	J	K	L
14												
15					Months before closing							
16			0	1	2	3	4					
17	Inverse of costs		0	22,500	56,250	67,500	78,750					
18												
19	Month		1	2	3	4	5	6 Total				
20	Remaining Periods		6	5	4	3	2	1				
21	Sales		0	0	0	0	1	1	2			
22			78,750	146,250	123,750	78,750	22,500	0				
23				=SUMPRODUCT($C$17:$G$17,D20:H20)								
24				=SUMPRODUCT(OFFSET($C$17,0,0,1,5),D20:H20)								
25				=SUMPRODUCT(OFFSET($C$17,0,0,1,MIN($G$16+1,C$20)),OFFSET(C21,0,0,1,MIN($G$16+1,C$20)))								
26			Total Costs		450,000							
27												

Note: the costs can occur over five months not four. We used zero for the month of sale. In our projection, we will use 1 as the month of sale.

Calculating Production Costs on the *Projection* Worksheet

Now we can enter our purchases on the cash flow forecast. Figure 5.15 shows the formula on the *Projection* sheet in cell B21.

Figure 5.15 The purchases formula on the *Projection* sheet

		B22	▾	*fx*	=SUMPRODUCT(OFFSET(Assumptions!$L$7,0,0,1,MIN(Assumptions!$L$5,B$5)),OFFSET(B$8,0,0,1,MIN(Assumptions!$L$5,B$5)))

	A	B	C	D	E	F	G	H	I	J	K	L	M	N	O	P
22	Purchases	0	78,750	225,000	348,750	506,250	517,500	427,500	326,250	168,750	78,750	22,500	0	2,700,000		

The formula in B22 is:

=SUMPRODUCT(OFFSET(Assumptions!$L$7,0,0,1,MIN(Assumptions!$L$5,B$5)),OFFSET(B$8,0,0,1,MIN(Assumptions!$L$5,B$5)))

That formula is copied from B22:M22. Copy it from the file and play with it. A lot of times you learn by busting things like this formula.

Adding Functions that Contain Logic

Now, let's assume we have to make a deposit on the land. Once again, open the Chapter 5_Production Costs workbook at www.nahb.org/financialforecasting. On the *Assumptions* sheet, there is now a Misc. Assumptions box. In cell B13, type in the formula: =B7*5000. This says we will deposit $5,000 for each lot (fig 5.16). In cell B14, type "P3."

Figure 5.16 Creating a deposit on the land

	A	B
12	**Misc. Assumptions**	
13	Deposit on Land	60,000
14	Period deposit due	3
15	Date Due	Sep-14

In cell B15, we are going to create the due date for our land deposit by using the formula: =EOMONTH(B5,B14), which takes the date in B5 (Jun-14) and offsets it by the number of months in B14 (3) and returns the end of the month value (Sep-14—internally it is the value September 30, 2014, but we formatted the cell to show just the month and year).

We could also have taken the reverse approach, by entering the date that the deposit is due and calculating the period in which the payment is due:

- To calculate the number of months or periods between two dates, our formula would be: **=(YEAR(B11)-YEAR(B5))*12 +MONTH(B11)-MONTH(B5)+1** B11and B5 contain the 2 dates. Note: I find it easier to work with periods instead of dates; it makes my formulas less cumbersome.

- This formula does not use the day of the month in its calculation. For example, given a start date of 10/31/00 and an end date of 11/2/00, one month is returned even though only two days elapsed.

- The number that is returned equals the number of months from the start date of the projection to the end date, rounded up to the next whole number.

IF Function

The **IF** function is a formula that asks Excel to test a specific condition that you specify. If the condition is True, it returns one value and a different value if the condition is False. You can think of this as "If this is true, then X; if this is false then Y." The syntax of an IF statement is as follows: **=IF(logical test, value if true, [value if false])**

To test if cell A1 = 2. We would write the formula: **=IF(A1=2,60000,0)**. That means if the value of cell A1 is 2, then the value in which this formulas resides is 60,000 (12 lots × a down payment of \$5,000 per lot = \$60,000) otherwise it is 0.

To test if A1 ≠ 2, the formula would change to: **=IF(A1< > 2,0,60000)**. Again, this is read as: If the value of cell A1 is not 2, the cell value is 0; otherwise the cell value is 60,000. Note: In Excel, use the less-than sign (<) followed by the the greater-than sign (>) to indicate "not equal to" (≠).

To test if A1 ≥ 2, the formula would be: **=IF(A1>= 2,60000,0)**. This reads as: If the value of cell A1 is greater than or equal to 2, the value for the resident cell (the cell in which the formula resides) is 60,000; otherwise it is 0. When typing out this formula, make sure to type > and then =, in that order. The equal sign goes last. If you mistype it, you will get an error warning.

When you use text value in a formula rather than a number, you need put the value in quotation marks. For example, the formula: **=IF(A1="Feb",60000,0)** means that if the value of cell A1 is "Feb" then the value in which this formula resides is 60,000, otherwise it is 0. The same is true if the text value is in the True or False part of the syntax. So, this formula : **=IF(A1=1,"Jan",8)** states that if the value of cell A1 is equal to 1 then the value in which this formula resides is "Jan," otherwise it is 0.

Finally, if you want either the True or False value to be an empty cell, the formula is **=IF(A1=1,,8)** or **=IF(A1=1,"",8)**. This means that if the value of cell A1 is equal to 1, then the value in which the formula resides is an empty cell, otherwise it is 8. Note: To indicate the empty cell, use two commas in a row or two quotation marks in a row—with not even a space in between.

IF, AND, and OR

You may set more than one condition and link them with AND/OR. Write all the conditions separated by commas within a set of parentheses, like so: **=AND(first condition, second condition, etc.)**

Using AND/OR is easy, as it allows you to create multiple conditions. Suppose we need to pay $5,000 in overhead from the second period until the last period of the pro forma. (The length of pro forma [in months] is on the *Assumptions* page in cell B6.)

The formula: **=IF(AND(A1>=2,A1<=12),5000,0)** means that if the value of cell A1 is greater than or equal to 2 *and* less than or equal to 12, then the value of the cell 5,000, otherwise it is 0. In order for the formula to return 5000, the value in cell A1 must respect *both* conditions.

The formula: **=IF(OR(A1=1,A1=12),5000,0)** means that if the value of cell A1 is equal to 1 *or* 12, the value of the cell is 5,000, otherwise it is 0. In this case, 5,000 is returned for any value that respects either one of the conditions.

IF (Nested)

What if there are multiple conditions and outcomes? Suppose you want to have a value of 60,000 if it is month one, and if it is between months 2 and 12, you want 5,000, and 0 for anything else For this set of conditions the formula is: **=IF(A1=1, 60000,IF(AND(A1>=2,A1<=12),5000,0)).**

Notice that there are the same number of closing parentheses as opening parentheses, and there is one closing parentheses for each if statement.

Now click on the *Projection* sheet so that we can add our deposit to our cash flow statement.

- Highlight row 21 and then simultaneously press **Ctrl +** to create another row. Note: All row formulas will adjust automatically based on the way we set up the SUM formulas.

- In cell A21, type *Land Deposit.*

- **Copy** cell N22 and **Paste** it into cell N21.

- We can use one of two methods here:

  - **=IF(Assumptions!$B$14=B4,Assumptions!$B$13,0)** says that if the period on the *Assumptions* page cell B14 (in this case, period 3) is the same as the period in cell B4, then insert the value $60,000 (from cell B13 on the *Assumptions* page), otherwise use 0.

- We could have also used this formula: **=IF(EOMONTH(Assumptions! $B$15,0)=B$8,Assumptions!$B$13,0)**. This says that if the end of the month on the *Assumptions* page B15 (Sept. 1, 2014) matches the end of the month on line B8 (recall line 8 uses the EOMONTH formula as well), then put in the value of $60,000 from the *Assumptions* page in cell B13.
- Both formulas give you the same results but the first one is more succinct.

Figure 5.17 a partial picture of our cash flow forecast:

Figure 5.17 The cash flow statement showing land deposits and construction costs

	B	C	D	E	F	G	H	I	J	K	L	M	N
10 Cash Balance - First of the Month	0	0	-78,750	-363,750	-712,500	-1,218,750	-1,436,250	-1,263,750	-990,000	-258,750	262,500	540,000	0
11													
12 Receipts:													
13 Construction Loan Draws													0
14 Closings	0	0	0	0	0	300,000	600,000	600,000	900,000	600,000	300,000	300,000	3,600,000
15 Collection on Receivables													
16 Deposits by Customers													0
17													0
18 Total Cash Receipts	0	0	0	0	0	300,000	600,000	600,000	900,000	600,000	300,000	300,000	3,600,000
19													
20 Disbursements													
21 Land Deposit	0	0	60,000	0	0	0	0	0	0	0	0	0	60,000
22 Purchases	0	78,750	225,000	348,750	506,250	517,500	427,500	326,250	168,750	78,750	22,500	0	2,700,000
23 Indirect Construction Costs													
24 Financing Costs (Interest)													0
25 Marketing Costs													0
26 General & Administrative Costs													0
27 Construction Loan Repayments													0
28													
29 Total Disbursements	0	78,750	285,000	348,750	506,250	517,500	427,500	326,250	168,750	78,750	22,500	0	2,760,000
30													
31 Net cash flow for month	0	-78,750	-285,000	-348,750	-506,250	-217,500	172,500	273,750	731,250	521,250	277,500	300,000	840,000
32													
33 Cash Excess (Shortage)	0	-78,750	-363,750	-712,500	-1,218,750	-1,436,250	-1,263,750	-990,000	-258,750	262,500	540,000	840,000	840,000
34 Funds Needed													0
35 Cash Distributions													0
36													
37 Cash Balance - End of Month	0	-78,750	-363,750	-712,500	-1,218,750	-1,436,250	-1,263,750	-990,000	-258,750	262,500	540,000	840,000	840,000

The timing of construction costs is one of the biggest factors that affects cash flow. Careful attention to the details can make or break a project. Avoid being too optimistic in your construction schedule or cost controls. Review your pricing, and make certain that you can hit the gross profit margins you expect. If the project is on time and within budget, you'll make the money you expect. But if the project costs more and takes more time, not only will your margins go down, but your other overhead costs will go up as well. For example, if it takes an extra three months to build—your interest costs go up and so do your marketing costs.

Budgeting Overhead Costs

6

The hard work is pretty much done, but we have only discussed the first three steps. We still have four steps to go. The fourth step covers how to budget for overhead costs. While there are many different methods to deal with overhead, this book will cover just one.

Step 4. Budget Your Overhead Costs

The Wall Street Approach

Most planners determine their cost of overhead with certain specified levels of operations. Traditionally, the accounting equation dictates that Revenue – Costs of Goods Sold – Overhead = Profits. That is the way most businesses operate. However, this is reactive and doesn't let you control the business. Look at the way Wall Street operates: Revenue – Profits = Expenses. This says that whatever is left after you "make money" and pay for production costs can be allocated to run the company. This is very proactive.

Let me offer an alternative: budget overhead levels based upon basic planning ratios. For example:

- Cost of Sales: 75% of sales
- Overhead: 15% of sales
- Profit (before taxes): 10% of sales
- You can then break down the 15% overhead into subcategories:
- Indirect Construction Costs: 2.5% of sales
- Finance Costs: 4.5% of sales
- Marketing Costs: 4.0% of sales
- General & Admin. Costs: 4.0% of sales

You can break down each of these subcategories further still. The 2.5% indirect construction costs could be broken down like so:

- Superintendent Salaries: 2.0% of sales
- Warranty Costs: 0.3% of sales
- Other Indirect Construction Costs: 0.2% of sales

Overhead Assumptions

For purposes of our projection in the Chapter 6_Budgeting Overhead Costs workbook at www.nahb.org/financialforecasting, let's structure our costs in accordance with the above schedule. In figure 6.1, I've inserted some rows and set column B23:B26 equal to a percentage of sales. Columns C and D, include the beginning months of the expenditures and the ending months (as some expenses aren't incurred equally throughout the pro forma periods). Again, we use formulas rather than hard numbers to allow for inevitable changes down the line. Finally, I created a monthly amount over the forecasted period.

Figure 6.1 The projection now includes added cost information.

	A	B	C	D	E
21	**Other Costs**				
22			From Per.	To Per.	
23	Indirect Construction Costs	2.5%	1	12	7,500
24	Financing Costs (Interest)	4.5%	1	12	13,500
25	Marketing Costs	4.0%	2	11	14,400
26	General & Administrative Costs	4.0%	1	12	12,000
27	Total Other Costs	15.0%			

Figure 6.2 shows the formulas in the cells.

Figure 6.2 The same area of the projection showing all the formulas.

	A	B	C	D	E
22			From Per.	To Per.	
23	Indirect Construction Costs	0.025	1	=$B$6	=($B23*$B$7*$B$8)/(D23-C23+1)
24	Financing Costs (Interest)	0.045	1	=$B$6	=($B24*$B$7*$B$8)/(D24-C24+1)
25	Marketing Costs	0.04	2	=$B$6-1	=($B25*$B$7*$B$8)/(D25-C25+1)
26	General & Administrative Costs	0.04	1	=$B$6	=($B26*$B$7*$B$8)/(D26-C26+1)
27	Total Other Costs	=SUM(B23:B26)			

Look at the formula in column E. It says: take the product of the percentage of sales in column B times the number of units times the average sales price (the percent of total sales) and divide it by the number of periods (the ending period – the beginning period + 1 month [to include the beginning month]). This equation gives us our average monthly costs over the relevant period.

Putting Overhead in the Projection

Now, it's time to bring our overhead numbers into the *Projection* sheet. Based on the scenarios above, we want to test whether the period on line B4 is greater than or equal to the beginning period on the *Assumptions* page in C23 and less than or equal to the ending period on the *Assumptions* page in D23. If it meets *both* those criteria, then we want the value in column E, row 16. The formula looks like this:

=IF(AND(B$4>=Assumptions!$C23,B$4<=Assumptions!$D23),
Assumptions!$E23,0)

Notice the use of the absolute reference markers. The first assumptions section in the formula (Assumptions!$C23) has only one absolute reference—the column. The row is flexible so that we only need to copy the formula down to lines 24, 25, and 26; these are for financing costs, marketing costs, and general & administrative costs respectively. The formulas for those lines look are as follows:

B24: =IF(AND(B$4>=Assumptions!$C24,B$4<=Assumptions!$D24),
Assumptions!$E24,0)

B25: =IF(AND(B$4>=Assumptions!$C25,B$4<=Assumptions!$D25),
Assumptions!$E25,0)

B26: =IF(AND(B$4>=Assumptions!$C26,B$4<=Assumptions!$D26),
Assumptions!$E26,0)

Compare the formulas and look what changed and what stayed the same. By using these formulas, we create efficiencies of programming as well as efficiencies in changing constants (fig 6.3).

Figure 6.3 The *Projection* worksheet with more cost assumptions filled in

	A	B	C	D	E	F
4	Period	1	2	3	4	5
23	Indirect Construction Costs	7,500	7,500	7,500	7,500	7,500
24	Financing Costs (Interest)	13,500	13,500	13,500	13,500	13,500
25	Marketing Costs	0	14,400	14,400	14,400	14,400
26	General & Administrative Costs	12,000	12,000	12,000	12,000	12,000

Notice that you can see lines 4 and 24, 25, and 26. You can do this by freezing panes (see Chapter 1, page 13).

Your hard work should be paying off now. This chapter was more about formatting and saving time than it was about programming. Once you become acquainted with these shortcuts, your skills will quickly improve.

Deposits, Loans, Accounts Receivable

We've now covered income and expenses in the conventional accounting format. But money can flow into your project from a variety of other sources. In this chapter we will cover Step 5, which explores those sources that usually show up on a balance sheet, not an income statement. We will get to the financial statements in Chapter 10, but creating a cash flow projection first aligns better with the way a business owner thinks.

Step 5. Determine Other Sources of Funds

- Determine when you will receive the draws from your lenders for the jobs. Then include all other sources of cash of a routine nature (e.g., land sales, sale of warehouse, deposits, etc.)
- Loans
- Investors
- Customer Deposits
- Collections on accounts receivable (A/R)

Loans

The logic behind fitting loans into your cash flow forecast is essentially like calculating your construction costs except that you may not be able to borrow 100% of your costs. Your objective is to match cash outflows for construction (building your project) to cash inflows during construction.

We add column C to the *Assumptions* sheet in the Chapter 7_Deposits Loans Accounts Receivable workbook at www.nahb.org/financialforecasting (figure 7.1).

Figure 7.1 The *Assumptions* sheet with a Borrowings column

	A	B	C
29	**Purchases/Borrowings**		
30		Purchases	Borrowings
31	Month of Sale	0.0%	0.0%
32	1 Month before sale	10.0%	10.0%
33	2 Months before sale	25.0%	25.0%
34	3 Months before sale	30.0%	30.0%
35	4 Months before sale	35.0%	15.0%
36	5 Months before sale	0.0%	0.0%
37	6 Months before sale	0.0%	0.0%
38	Total	100.0%	80.0%

Our assumption on line 38 is that we can only borrow 80% of costs, and in month one, we can only borrow 15% of total costs (35% less the 20% equity required), not the full 35% of amount borrowed (line 38).

Figure 7.2 shows that we have expanded our costs and borrowings table and added the range K8:S9. Note: we have to manually insert the percentages of cost that we can borrow and the timing of those costs.

Figure 7.2   Additional costs have been added to the worksheet.

	K	L	M	N	O	P	Q	R	S
3	Costs and borrowings								
4		Months before sale							Constr.
5	Months before the sale	7	6	5	4	3	2	1	Months
6	Inverse (in percent)	0%	10%	25%	30%	35%	0%	0	100%
7	Schedule of costs incurred	0	22,500	56,250	67,500	78,750	0	0	225,000
8	Amount Loaned (Inverse)	0%	10%	25%	30%	15%	0%	0	80%
9	Schedule of amounts borrowed	0	22,500	56,250	67,500	33,750	0	0	180,000

Figure 7.3 shows the formulas for this same section:

Figure 7.3 The same section of the worksheet, now with the formulas shown.

	K	L	M	N	O	P	Q	R	S
3	Costs and borrowings								
4		Months before sale							Constr.
5	Months before the sale	7	=L5-1	=M5-1	=N5-1	=O5-1	=P5-1	=Q5-1	Months
6	Inverse (in percent)	=+B31	=+B32	=+B33	=+B34	=+B35	=+B36	=+C37	=SUM(L6:R6)
7	Schedule of costs incurred	=$B$9*L6	=$B$9*M6	=$B$9*N6	=$B$9*O6	=$B$9*P6	=$B$9*Q6	=$B$9*R6	=SUM(L7:R7)
8	Amount Loaned (Inverse)	=+C31	=+C32	=+C33	=+C34	=+C35	=+C36	=+C37	=SUM(L8:R8)
9	Schedule of amounts borrowed	=$B$9*L8	=$B$9*M8	=$B$9*N8	=$B$9*O8	=$B$9*P8	=$B$9*Q8	=$B$9*R8	=SUM(L9:R9)

Line 9 takes the average cost of a unit (S7) and multiplies it by the appropriate borrowing percentage. You could add a formula to check to make sure that the amount you borrow isn't in excess of what you are allowed to borrow. If the average cost per unit (B9) multiplied by the amount you can borrow (80% on line B9) minus the calculated amount you can borrow on line S9 equals zero (in other words, the amounts are equal) then put in a blank space. If they aren't equal, let the cell show the word "error." In cell T9 the test formula looks like this: **=IF(-SUM(L9:R9)=S9,"0","error")**. I like "0" as that is an easy number to see versus looking at two numbers and relying on your eyes to see that they are equal.

Now let's get this into our cash flow statement. Click on the *Projection* sheet. The formula is exactly the same as on line 22 for purchases (see Chapter 5 Scheduling Your Production Costs, page 41):

=SUMPRODUCT(OFFSET(Assumptions! $L$7,0,0,1,MIN(Assumptions! $L$5,B$5)),OFFSET(B$8,0,0,1,MIN(Assumptions!$L$5,B$5))).

Except now our reference is to $L$9 (instead of $L$7) for the first OFFSET (which is the amount you can *borrow* not the purchases you incur):

=SUMPRODUCT(OFFSET(Assumptions! $L$9,0,0,1,MIN(Assumptions! $L$5,B$5)),OFFSET(B$8,0,0,1,MIN(Assumptions!$L$5,B$5))).

In order to set this up, click on the formula in B22. **Copy** the formula and **Paste** it to line 13. Hit the **F2 key** in order to edit the formula. Move your cursor to $L$7 and replace it with $L$9 and hit **Enter**. Then **drag** the formula over to column N.

Figure 7.4 shows that the total borrowings in cell N13 are $2,160,000 or 80% of your average costs of $2,700,000.

Figure 7.4 Cell N13 now calculates the borrowings as 80% of cell N22.

	A	B	C	D	E	F	G	H	I	J	K	L	M	N
4	Period	1	2	3	4	5	6	7	8	9	10	11	12	
6	Month	Jun-14	Jul-14	Aug-14	Sep-14	Oct-14	Nov-14	Dec-14	Jan-15	Feb-15	Mar-15	Apr-15	May-15	Total
7	Year	2014	2014	2014	2014	2014	2014	2014	2015	2015	2015	2015	2015	
8	Sales in Units						1	2	2	3	2	1	1	12
9														
10	Cash Balance - First of the Month	0	-33,000	-125,400	-322,800	-451,200	-615,600	-444,000	72,600	580,200	1,414,800	1,958,400	2,202,000	0
11														
12	Receipts:													
13	Construction Loan Draws	0	33,750	135,000	258,750	371,250	427,500	382,500	281,250	168,750	78,750	22,500	0	2,160,000
14	Closings	0	0	0	0	0	300,000	600,000	600,000	900,000	600,000	300,000	300,000	3,600,000
15	Collection on Receivables	0	0	0	0	0	0	0	0	0	0	0	0	0
16	Deposits by Customers	0	0	0	9,000	18,000	9,000	9,000	0	-18,000	-9,000	-9,000	-9,000	0
17														
18	Total Cash Receipts	0	33,750	135,000	267,750	389,250	736,500	991,500	881,250	1,050,750	669,750	313,500	291,000	5,760,000
19														
20	Disbursements													
21	Land Deposit	0	0	60,000	0	0	0	0	0	0	0	0	0	60,000
22	Purchases	0	78,750	225,000	348,750	506,250	517,500	427,500	326,250	168,750	78,750	22,500	0	2,700,000

Customer Deposits

Customer deposits represent short-term sources of cash. They are typically a balance sheet item, in that their receipt is a liability and at closing, they are applied to a sale. At the end of a project, the effect of deposits is zero.

In order to use deposits in a pro forma, we will insert two more lines in the assumptions. We could use a fixed-dollar amount for the deposit or a percentage. Using a percentage allows you to change the average price assumption and have the deposits adjust automatically. (Remember, one of our rules for programming is to make a change in one place and have it carry over to wherever there may be a formulaic relationship between numbers.)

Our first step is to create the assumptions related to deposits. We do this on the *Assumptions* sheet. We are going to add some information to the Misc. Assumptions section of our *Assumptions* sheet (specifically, lines 16 and 17 in figure 7.5).

Figure 7.5 Misc. Assumptions box on the *Assumptions* sheet

	A	B
12	**Misc. Assumptions**	
13	Deposit on Land	60,000
14	Period deposit due	3
15	Date Due	Sep-14
16	Deposits	3%
17	Deposit prepayment (in months)	2
18	Cash Contingency	100,000
19	Safety Cash	50,000

The deposit will be calculated at 3% of the sales price, and on average, we will collect the deposits (get a contract on the unit) two months before the closing. Obviously, once you create parameters (constants, or variables), you can change them at will, knowing that the balance of your pro forma will adjust accordingly. This allows for a strong "what if" analysis.

Now go to the *Projection* sheet, line 16 "Deposits by Customers." The logic is: If the remaining period is greater than the deposit prepayments in months (you can't have a deposit in the last two months of the projection because theoretically a sale can't happen beyond the projection period) then take the deposit percentage (3% on cell B16) times the average sales price (Assumptions!$B$8) times the number of closings expected two months out (offset the current month sales on line 8 by the number of months that we collect a deposit in advance). If we are at the end of our projection, we will not get a deposit so use 0:

=IF(B$5>Assumptions!$B$17,Assumptions!$B$16*Assumptions!$B$8*
OFFSET(B$8,0,Assumptions!$B$17),0).

But we have to adjust the formula so that as we have the closings, the deposits are applied to the sales price. That formula would look like this:

$$\text{=-B8*Assumptions!\$B\$8*Assumptions!\$B\$13.}$$

This tells Excel to subtract the current month sales times the average sales price times the percentage deposit taken. Now combine the two thoughts into one formula:

$$\text{=IF(B\$5>Assumptions!\$B\$17,Assumptions!\$B\$16*Assumptions!\$B\$8*}$$
$$\text{OFFSET(B\$8,0,Assumptions!\$B\$17),0)-B8*Assumptions!\$B\$8*}$$
$$\text{Assumptions!\$B\$16.}$$

The net effect of deposits in cell N16 is zero (fig 7.6). That's because all customer deposits are applied to a closing (as it should be).

Figure 7.6 Deposits by customers reveals the timing of deposits and their application to the actual sale.

	A	B	C	D	E	F	G	H	I	J	K	L	M	N
4	Period	1	2	3	4	5	6	7	8	9	10	11	12	
5	Remaining Periods	12	11	10	9	8	7	6	5	4	3	2	1	
6	Month	Jun-14	Jul-14	Aug-14	Sep-14	Oct-14	Nov-14	Dec-14	Jan-15	Feb-15	Mar-15	Apr-15	May-15	Total
8	Sales in Units						1	2	2	3	2	1	1	12
9														
10	Cash Balance - First of the Mon	0	-33,000	-125,400	-322,800	-451,200	-615,600	-444,000	72,600	580,200	1,414,800	1,958,400	2,202,000	0
11														
12	Receipts:													
13	Construction Loan Draws	0	33,750	135,000	258,750	371,250	427,500	382,500	281,250	168,750	78,750	22,500	0	2,160,000
14	Closings	0	0	0	0	0	300,000	600,000	600,000	900,000	600,000	300,000	300,000	3,600,000
15	Collection on Receivables	0	0	0	0	0	0	0	0	0	0	0	0	0
16	Deposits by Customers	0	0	0	9,000	18,000	9,000	9,000	0	-18,000	-9,000	-9,000	-9,000	0

Collections on Receivables

The logic of collections of receivables is very similar to the purchases discussion, but purchases are based on future events; you have to start construction and pay for construction before the sales date. Accounts receivable are based on past events; you made a sale and will collect on it in future periods. In homebuilding, you will usually collect all proceeds at closing. However, if you are a remodeler (for instance) you may get progress payments. This changes your cash flow.

Assume that you have sales as shown in figure 7.7.

Figure 7.7 Hypothetical sales schedule

	A	B	C	D	E	F	G	H	I
1	Period		1	2	3	4	5	6	7
2	Sales		100	200	300	400	500	0	0

(This is an illustration only and is not on the spreadsheet, but included here to show you how this evolves.) Further assume that 25% of your sales are cash sales (or you collect 25% of the sales in the first month) and the balance of 75% comes in month two. Then your cash flow would look like figure 7.8.

Figure 7.8 Timing of cash flows

	A	B	C	D	E	F	G	H	I
1	Period		1	2	3	4	5	6	7
2	Sales		100	200	300	400	500	0	0
3									
4	Collections:								
5	Current month collection:	25%	25	50	75	100	125	0	0
6	Next month collections	75%		75	150	225	300	375	0
7		....	....	....	....	....	....	....	....
8	Total Collections		25	125	225	325	425	375	0

As you add a longer and longer receivable cycle, this calculation gets more and more complex. So once again, we input the percent of revenues collected in the appropriate month (in other words the collection cycle) in figure 7.9.

Figure 7.9 The collection cycle

	K	L	M	N	O	P	Q	R	S
12	Accounts Receivable								
13		Collections (months after sale (0 is the month of sale))							Collection
14	Months before the sale	0	1	2	3	4	5	6	Months
15	% of Revenue	25%	75%	0%	0%	0%	0%	0%	
16	Inverse (in percent)	0%	0%	0%	0%	0%	75%	25%	2

This is identical to the discussion of purchases. So, our single formula would be to take the SUMPRODUCT of the sales times the amount collected for the corresponding month. We want 25% of the current month and 75% of the preceding month. Thus, we depart from the discussion of purchases. We are now working in the past. So the offsets are going to include past columns and therefore, the sign on the offset will be negative:

=SUMPRODUCT(OFFSET(C$2,0,0,1,-2),OFFSET($H$14,0,0,1,-2)).

This reads: The current cell value equals the SUMPRODUCT of the current sales (C$2) as well as the preceding month (thus the minus two instead of a positive two) times the current month collections plus the preceding months' collections.

Once again, the problem of the starting the calculation before the projection begins appears. So we have to use the MIN function to make sure we don't derive collections from periods before the projections appear. This requires the following adjustment to the last parameter of the OFFSET function:

$$=MIN(C\$1,\$I\$14).$$

This goes back a minimum of the collection period or the current period number. So our revised formula looks like this:

$$=SUMPRODUCT(OFFSET(C\$2,0,0,1,-MIN(C\$1,\$I\$14)),$$
$$OFFSET(\$H\$14,0,0,1,-MIN(C\$1,\$I\$14))).$$

Again, note the negative signs before the MIN function. TIP: Make sure that you have enough periods after the sale to get all your receipts.

Now, back to our projection. Add the information shown in figure 7.10 to the Accounts Receivable box on the *Assumptions* page.

Figure 7.10 The collection cycle in our *Projection* worksheet

	A	B
40	**Accounts Receivable**	
41	Cash Collections	100.0%
42	30 days for collection	0.0%
43	60 days for collection	0.0%
44	90 days for collection	0.0%
45	120 days for collection	0.0%
46	180 days for collection	0.0%
47	210 days for collection	0.0%
48	Total	100.0%

Then link the information in figure 7.10 to the Accounts Receivable box (fig 7.11).

Figure 7.11 The Accounts Receivable box aligns the collection cycle for the OFFSET command.

	K	L	M	N	O	P	Q	R	S
12	Accounts Receivable								
13		Collections (months after sale (0 is the month of sale))							Collection
14	Months before the sale	0	1	2	3	4	5	6	Months
15	% of Revenue	100%	0%	0%	0%	0%	0%	0%	
16	Inverse (in percent)	0%	0%	0%	0%	0%	0%	100%	1

The formulas are shown in figure 7.12.

Figure 7.12 Formulas for the Accounts Receivable box

	K	L	M	N	O	P	Q	R	S
12	Accounts Receivable								
13		Collections (months after sale (0 is the month of sale))							Collection
14	Months before the sale	0	=L14+1	=M14+1	=N14+1	=O14+1	=P14+1	=Q14+1	Months
15	% of Revenue	=+B41	=+B42	=+B43	=+B44	=+B45	=+B46	=1-SUM(L1	
16	Inverse (in percent)	=+R15	=+Q15	=+P15	=+O15	=+N15	=+M15	=+L15	=COUNTIF(L16:R16,">0")

On the *Projection* page (line 14), adjust the formulas for cash sales to multiply the sales price by the amount collected in $R$16 (note the absolute reference). Cash collections will now be sales times average price times collections in the month of sale ($H$60 – an absolute reference).

Now, let's create the formulas for the "Collections on Receivables" line (line 15 on the *Projection* page). Initially, we need to multiply the number of sales (the first OFFSET command) by the collection cycle (the second OFFSET command in the formula below):

=SUMPRODUCT(OFFSET(B$8,0,0,1,-MIN(B$1,Assumptions!$S$16)),
OFFSET(Assumptions!$R$16,0,0,1,-MIN(B$1,Assumptions!$S$16))).

Then we need to multiply the results by the average price from the *Assumptions* sheet in cell B8 and reduce that amount by any collections on line 14 or: *Assumptions!$B$8-B14,0). So the formula is:

=SUMPRODUCT(OFFSET(B$8,0,0,1,
-MIN(B$1,Assumptions!$S$16)),OFFSET(Assumptions!$R$16,0,0,1,
-MIN(B$1,Assumptions!$S$16)))*Assumptions!$B$8-B14.

The formulas are on line 14 of the *Projection* sheet in the Chapter 7_Deposits Loans Accounts Recivable workbook.

OK, let out a sigh of relief. If you are selling homes, you probably won't need this formula. But if you are receiving progress payments, this could get a little trickier.

COUNT, COUNTA, and COUNTIF Functions

In cell S16 on the *Assumptions* page, you may have noticed a function that starts with COUNTIF. Let's describe those functions for counting numbers in a range.

The COUNT function counts the number of cells that contain numbers in a range. The syntax is as follows: **=COUNT(range)**.

The argument is the range of cells to be used. The COUNT function ignores empty cells or non-numeric cells in a range. If you add a number in the range, the count total is updated automatically.

For example, you can enter the following formula to count the numbers in the range A1:A10: **=COUNT(A1:A10)**. In this example, if five of the cells in the range contain numbers, the result is 5.

The COUNTA function only counts non-blank cells that contain data such as text, numbers, or formulas. It will ignore blank or empty cells in a range. The syntax for this formula is: **=COUNTA(range)**. The argument is the range of cells to be used.

The COUNTIF function is used to count the number of times specific data is found in a selected group of cells. The syntax is: **=COUNTIF(range, criteria)**. For example, if you wanted to count all the values the range A1:A10 greater than 10, you would create the following formula: **=COUNTIF(A1:A10,">10")**.

Note the quotation marks around the criteria. The criteria argument is in the form of a number, expression, or text that defines which cells will be counted. For example, criteria can be expressed as 20, "20", "=20", ">20", "North", "N*". COUNTIF will work on data such as text and numbers.

In figure 7.11, cell S16 contained a formula that says: count all cells in the range L16:R16 that have a value greater than 0 and add 1 month. This will give us the collection timeframe, assuming you close in the month following the completion of construction. The syntax for the formula is: **=COUNTIF(L16:R16,">0")**.

At this point, all receipts have been accounted for. There are many permutations of the formulas that we've used so far. For instance, if we have more periods, we'd simply insert columns before the total column. If we want to have variable pricing, we would add rows in the projection showing not only units sold but average sales price. We could inflate costs and inflate revenues. If you can ask the question, then you need to customize the spreadsheet to answer it.

Now, turn your attention to expenditures that aren't on the profit and loss statement.

Expenditures Not on Your Income Statement

8

Just as certain receipts never show up on the income statement, there are certain expenditures that don't show up on the income statement, either. Expenditures not included in the income statement include repayment of construction loans, payments for stakeholders (investors) and/or purchases of equipment or other capital expenditures. Again, it would pay to review the bucket theory in figure 1.1 on page 2.

Step 6. Determine What Expenses You'll Need to Pay that Aren't Shown on Your Income Statement

In this chapter we are going to focus on debt repayment. Purchases of capital equipment (long term assets) will not be covered as these are not usually significant costs in this particular type of pro forma. We'll cover distributions (or payments to investors) in Chapter 9 Equity Needs.

Debt Repayment

Loans Made on Each Individual Home

We borrowed money, now we have to pay it back. Projecting this is easy in comparison to incurring the debt. Every time there is a closing, we only need to pay back the amount we borrowed. Open workbook Chapter 8_Expenditures Not on Your Income Statement at www.nahb.org/financialforecasting. Recall that on the *Assumptions* page, we already calculated the amount borrowed per home in cell S9 (fig 8.1).

Figure 8.1   Construction loan draw schedule

	K	L	M	N	O	P	Q	R	S
3	Costs and borrowings								
4		Months before sale							Constr.
5	Months before the sale	7	6	5	4	3	2	1	Months
6	Inverse (in percent)	0%	10%	25%	30%	35%	0%	0	100%
7	Schedule of costs incurred	0	22,500	56,250	67,500	78,750	0	0	225,000
8	Amount Loaned (Inverse)	0%	10%	25%	30%	15%	0%	0	80%
9	Schedule of amounts borrowed	0	22,500	56,250	67,500	33,750	0	0	180,000
10									

We need to enter a formula into Construction Loan Repayments line (line 27) of the Cash Flow Statement on the *Projection* sheet. Starting in cell B27, the formula would be the number of closings multiplied by the amount we borrowed per home: =B8*Assumptions!$S$9.

After copying the formula from B27:M27, our spreadsheet would look like figure 8.2.

Figure 8.2   Construction loan repayments

	A	B	C	D	E	F	G	H	I	J	K	L	M	N
4	Period	1	2	3	4	5	6	7	8	9	10	11	12	
6	Month	Jun-14	Jul-14	Aug-14	Sep-14	Oct-14	Nov-14	Dec-14	Jan-15	Feb-15	Mar-15	Apr-15	May-15	Total
27	Construction Loan Repayments	0	0	0	0	0	198,000	396,000	396,000	594,000	396,000	180,000	0	2,160,000

Lines of Credit

If you have a line of credit rather than a construction loan, then the formula may get a little more complex. Let's set up our assumptions using the LOC Assumption box on the *Assumptions* sheet.

We are going to get a line of credit for 80% of our costs of construction. Our costs of construction are 12 units multiplied by $225,000 (B7*B9) or $2,700,000. Under the terms of the agreement with the financing entity, at every closing we have to pay the lesser of the balance of the loan, or 110% of the amounts borrowed per unit (i.e., $225,000*80% loan to cost*1.10) $198,000 at each closing. Remember you borrowed $180,000 per home ($225,000 cost times 80%). We also have to account for the 20% of the costs we would have to spend before the loan kicks in: $45,000 per home multiplied by 12 = $540,000 (fig 8.3).

Figure 8.3 Assumptions associated with a line of credit

	G	H
3	**LOC Assumption**	
4	Bank Financing	80%
5	Construction Costs	2,700,000
6	Loan Amount	2,160,000
7	Developer Contribution	540,000
8	Multiplier	1.10
9	Amont Paid per loan	198,000

We are borrowing an average of $180,000 per home (just like in our construction loan calculations), but instead of paying back $180,000, the bank requires us to pay this amount plus a 1.10 multiplier (or $198,000) every time a home closes. So taking this all into consideration, we want to do all this accounting below the cash flow statement.

Now let's turn to the *Projection* sheet lines 72 through 76. Figure 8.4 shows a partial view of what this section will look like.

Figure 8.4 Repaying a line of credit

	A	B	C	D	E	F	G	H
72	Cummulative Costs	0	78,750	303,750	652,500	1,158,750	1,676,250	2,103,750
73	Construction Loan - LOC	0	0	0	112,500	506,250	517,500	427,500
74	Repayments	0	0	0	0	0	198,000	396,000
75								
76	Repay loan	0	0	0	112,500	618,750	938,250	969,750

The following is another illustrative example only.

Line 72 is cumulative costs from line 22. In cell B72, the formula is: **=B22**. In line B72, it is: **=C22+B72**. This is the same as SUM($B$22:C22). Note that as we copy this formula over into other columns, B22 won't change but C22 will be the costs of the current column.

Line 73 calculates how much we can borrow. The first month is fairly easy as the only purchases are in month 1, and B22 is where all the construction costs are. Now we need to determine if we can borrow money or need to contribute equity. If the construction costs of this first month are less than the amount you (the developer) are required to contribute (Assumptions!$H$7), then you must contribute equity. If costs are greater than your contribution, then you will have to borrow the difference. The formula for this is:

$$=IF(B22<Assumptions!\$H\$7,0,B22-Assumptions!\$H\$7).$$

H7 is the developer contribution, and B22 is the current month's costs. But the second month, we need to look at the cumulative costs. We can borrow the minimum of the current costs—or cumulative costs less our equity contribution of $540,000. The formula would read like this:

=IF(SUM($B$22:C22)<Assumptions!$H$7,0,MIN(SUM($B$22:C22)
-Assumptions!$H$7,C22)).

If the costs to date, SUM($B$22:C22), are less than the developer's contribution (that is, *your* contribution), you can't borrow anything. (Note: the developer contribution will avoid all the other costs not considered "hard" costs by the lender. We'll cover that in equity contributions and distributions.)

If your costs are greater than your contribution, we can *only* fund the lesser (MIN) of our actual cost less the developers equity or the actual costs of that month:

=MIN(SUM($B$22:C22)-Assumptions!$H$7,C22).

Whatever we borrow would be linked to Construction Loan Draws (line 13) on the *Projection* sheet. The formula in line 13 would be replaced by: =B73. That formula would then be copied to columns C through M.

Next, when we pay back the line of credit, we have to pay the pro-rated amount borrowed for each home and a premium of 110% (Assumptions!$H$8) until the loan is paid back in full. So the amount you need to pay back is the number of closings times the loan per unit times the multiplier:

=Assumptions!$H$9*Projection!B$8.

However, applying this formula without regard to how much you've paid in the past can cause an overpayment. In order to rectify that, you have to look at the amount you borrowed and how much you've repaid. So, on line 76 below the debt analysis, we are going to calculate the outstanding loan balance that will eventually funnel into an income statement or balance sheet. It is the amount of the outstanding loan, which is the amount outstanding from the previous month plus the amount borrowed in the current month less payments. For month one, the amount is:

=B73-B74.

This is the current month's borrowings minus the current month loan repayments. For the next month and each month thereafter, it is:

=B76+C73-C74.

Line 76 is the line that tracks the loan's outstanding balance. We add the previous month's balance with the current month borrowings less the current month loan repayments. Now, when we have closings, the amount paid will be the lesser of the amount paid per loan (Assumptions!$H$9) or the loan balance from the previous month minus the amount borrowed in the current month:

=MIN(C8*Assumptions!$H$9,+B76+C73).

B76 is the outstanding loan balance of the previous month, and C73 is the amount borrowed in the current month.

To complete our substitution of a line of credit (verses the construction loan), we would then change the formulas on line 27. The repayment formula in cell 27 would be: **=B74.** We would then copy that formula to cells C74:M74.

The purpose of this example was to show another variation of paying back loans. We see the line of credit concept frequently when we build condominiums or townhomes.

We've only explored two variations of debt and its repayment. But the structuring of debt is limited only by your imagination. As you create your projection, make sure you account for money being borrowed, cumulative loans, repayment, and cumulative repayment. Again remember, anyone lending you money wants to make sure they get paid back with a fair return on their money.

Equity Needs

9

We've considered income and expenses, other sources of cash and other uses of cash that are not on the income statement. We've looked at the debt component of your projection. Now it is time to focus on the equity part (how much cash needs to go into your project) of your projection. Again, the methods of funding equity are only limited to your imagination. However, you must consider that investors want a return *on* their money and a return *of* their money. Your job is to convince them that both are possible.

This equity analysis is conducive to partnership taxation where distributions do not have to be equal.

Step 7. Determine Your Equity Needs and the Amount Will Pay Your Investors.

At this point, we know our costs, our revenues, cash flow from other sources, and cash expenditures to repay loans and purchase assets. Now, we need to know how much equity we need. To do that, we need two more commands: ROUNDUP and SUMIF.

ROUNDUP Function

The ROUNDUP function is used to round numbers up (whereas the ROUND function will round numbers up or down depending upon whether the last digit is greater than, less than, or equal to 5). The syntax for the ROUNDUP function is: =ROUNDUP(**Number, Num_digits**). Number is the value to be rounded, and Num_digits is the number of decimal places to reduce the above number to.

Figure 9.1 Using the ROUND, ROUNDUP and ROUNDDOWN functions

	A	B	C
1		5,621.35	5,651.35
2	Round -2	5,600.00	5,700.00
3	Round -1	5,620.00	5,650.00
4	Round 0	5,621.00	5,651.00
5	Round +1	5,621.40	5,651.40
6	Round+2	5,621.35	5,651.35
7			
8	Roundup -1	5,630.00	5,660.00
9	Roundup -2	5,700.00	5,700.00
10	Roundup 0	5,622.00	5,652.00
11	Roundup +1	5,621.40	5,651.40
12	Roundup +2	5,621.35	5,651.35
13			
14	Rounddown -1	5,620.00	5,650.00
15	Rounddown -2	5,600.00	5,600.00
16	Rounddown 0	5,621.00	5,651.00
17	Rounddown +1	5,621.30	5,651.30
18	Rounddown +2	5,621.35	5,651.35

Suppose we need to raise $5,621.35 in cell B1 and $5,651.35 in cell C1. In figure 9.1 we will use ROUND, ROUNDUP, and ROUNDDOWN to see the various results.

Figure 9.2 shows the formulas:

Figure 9.2 ROUND, ROUNDUP and ROUNDDOWN formulas associated with figure 9.1

	A	B	C
1		5621.35	5651.35
2	Round -2	=ROUND($B$1,-2)	=ROUND($C$1,-2)
3	Round -1	=ROUND($B$1,-1)	=ROUND($C$1,-1)
4	Round 0	=ROUND($B$1,0)	=ROUND($C$1,0)
5	Round +1	=ROUND($B$1,1)	=ROUND($C$1,1)
6	Round+2	=ROUND($B$1,2)	=ROUND($C$1,2)
7			
8	Roundup -1	=ROUNDUP($B$1,-1)	=ROUNDUP($C$1,-1)
9	Roundup -2	=ROUNDUP($B$1,-2)	=ROUNDUP($C$1,-2)
10	Roundup 0	=ROUNDUP($B$1,0)	=ROUNDUP($C$1,0)
11	Roundup +1	=ROUNDUP($B$1,1)	=ROUNDUP($C$1,1)
12	Roundup +2	=ROUNDUP($B$1,2)	=ROUNDUP($C$1,2)
13			
14	Rounddown -1	=ROUNDDOWN($B$1,-1)	=ROUNDDOWN(C$1,-1)
15	Rounddown -2	=ROUNDDOWN($B$1,-2)	=ROUNDDOWN($C$1,-2)
16	Rounddown 0	=ROUNDDOWN($B$1,0)	=ROUNDDOWN($C$1,0)
17	Rounddown +1	=ROUNDDOWN($B$1,1)	=ROUNDDOWN($C$1,1)
18	Rounddown +2	=ROUNDDOWN($B$1,2)	=ROUNDDOWN($C$1,2)

As you can see, the both the minus (or negative rounding) Num_digits and positive Num_digits round to the nearest tens, hundreds, thousands, etc. The Num_digits equal to zero rounds to the nearest dollar.

SUMIF Function

The SUMIF function is used to add the values in a list that meet criteria that you specify. Suppose that you want to add only the values that are less than zero in a row containing numbers. You can use the following formula: =SUMIF(B31:M31,"<0").

In this example, it looks for everything in the range B31:M31 that meets the criteria of being less than zero. Now let's apply this to our projection where we are trying to find out how much money we need on hand in order to make this project a success. Open the Chapter 9_Equity Needs workbook at www.nahb.org/financialforecasting and click on the *Projection* sheet.

The syntax for this function is: **=SUMIF (range, criteria, [sum_range])** Range is the group of cells that we want to evaluate (our criteria). Cells in each range must be numbers, names, arrays, or references that contain numbers. Blank and text values are ignored. The criteria are the identifiers for those cells, which will be added. If the criteria include logical or mathematical symbols, they must be enclosed in double quotation marks (") such as "<0".

Sum_range is an optional feature that allows you to look for a label in one row (or column) and add the number associated with that cell in another column. If the sum_range argument is omitted, Excel adds the cells that are specified in the range argument (the same cells to which the criteria are applied). For instance if you have a list of sales people in column A and their commissions in column B and you want the sum of all commissions paid to "John", the formula would be:

=SUMIF(A2:A25,"John",B2:B25).

Now, going back to our original: = SUMIF(B31:M31,"<0"), if we wanted to round it up to the nearest thousand dollars, our formula for ROUNDUP would be: =-ROUNDUP(Number,-3) Substituting our function for finding the amount of money we need our formula becomes:

=-ROUNDUP(SUMIF(B31:M31,"<0"),-3).

Note the negative sign in front of the formula. That is because we want an equity infusion that more than covers the negative cash flow. That is, we want to make sure we have enough money/available cash to cover the expenses we have to pay out along the way. But as it stands, this formula may not create enough cushion to ensure the success of the project. Planning conservatively, you might consider raising more money than you need to in order to cover contingencies. To do that, add a contingency amount, which is stated in line 18 of the Misc. Assumptions box on the *Assumptions* sheet (fig 9.3):

Figure 9.3 Cash contingency

	A	B
12	**Misc. Assumptions**	
13	Deposit on Land	60,000
14	Period deposit due	3
15	Date Due	Sep-14
16	Deposits	3%
17	Deposit prepayment (in months)	2
18	Cash Contingency	100,000
19	Safety Cash	50,000

Our final formula looks like this:

=-ROUNDUP(SUMIF(B31:M31,"<0"),-3)+Assumptions!$B$18.

Thus, we've created the formula to determine the amount of cash we need (the sum of all the months with negative cash flow) rounded up to the nearest $1,000 (giving us a little cushion for error) and then added $100,000 to allow us a larger cushion of error.

In our projection, on the *Projection* sheet in cell B34, we use the formula:

=-ROUNDUP(SUMIF(B31:M31,"<0"),-5)+Assumptions!$B$18.

Note that in cell B34, we ROUNDUP to the nearest $100,000 (-5). This formula says: take the sum of all monthly cash flows that are negative ("<0") and round up to the nearest $100,000 and then add the cash contingency to it. In cell C34, we have the formula:

=IF(AND(C4<Assumptions!$B$6,C33<Assumptions!$B$19),
Assumptions!$B$19-C33,0).

If our current period is less than the ending month of the projection and our cash balance (line 33 of the *Projection* sheet) is less than our safety cash (Assumptions!$B$19 – in this case $50,000), then we need to contribute the deficiency (Assumptions! !$B$19-C33).

TIP: I usually make cash contingency and safety cash the same number.

Cash Distributions

In theory, if there are no sales, then we can't distribute money. Sales are tallied on line 8 of the *Projection* sheet and using the formula: =SUM($B$8:B8). Note the use of the absolute reference to cell B8. In month 1, we are looking to see if there are any sales, but as we drag this formula to cell C35, the formula adjusts to: =SUM($B$8:C8). Remember, our objective is to create formulas that we can just drag—without having to adjust it for each cell—in order to expand our base.

If there are no sales, then we distribute no cash, so our partial formula is:

=-IF(SUM($B$8:B8)=0,0,

The negative in front of the equation shows a payment or distribution versus a receipt.

Now we need another test that says that if this is the last month of the projection, whatever the cash is (which can be both positive and negative) it gets distributed. Obviously if cash is negative at the end of the project, it means the builder/developer will have to ante up some money. We test the period on line 4 of the *Projection* sheet. If it equals the last month of the projection (Assumptions!$B$6), then we need to distribute whatever is left. Again, continuing on with our formula:

=-IF(SUM($B$8:B8)=0,0,IF(B4=Assumptions!$B$6,+B33.

During the project, we want to distribute cash, but we want "safety cash"—a minimum amount of cash on hand as shown in cell B19 of figure 9.4.

Figure 9.4 Safety cash

	A	B
12	**Misc. Assumptions**	
13	Deposit on Land	60,000
14	Period deposit due	3
15	Date Due	Sep-14
16	Deposits	3%
17	Deposit prepayment (in months)	2
18	Cash Contingency	100,000
19	Safety Cash	50,000

Thus, we want to distribute the maximum of the cash balance minus the safety cash or zero. Suppose that the project generates $40,000 of cash. That amount is below our safety cash of $50,000 (and $40,000 minus safety cash of $50,000 would yield a negative $10,000). Therefore, the max of negative $10,000 or zero would be zero. But, if the project generated $75,000 of cash, then you could distribute the greater of $25,000 ($75,000 less than the safety cash of $50,000) or zero. Thus, you could distribute $25,000 without having to touch your $50,000 in safety cash.

So, our final formula is:

$$\text{=-IF(SUM(\$B\$8:B8)=0,0,IF(B4=Assumptions!\$B\$6,+B33,MAX-}$$
$$\text{(B33+B34-Assumptions!\$B\$19,0))).}$$

This says:

- If we haven't had any sales, don't distribute any cash.

- If this is the last month of our projection, distribute the amount on line 33. Note: if this is negative it will drive another capital contribution.

- If there have been sales and this isn't the last month, distribute any cash on hand over our "safety cash" amount.

Once again, the only time all cash is distributed is at the end of the project.

So now we've determined how much needs to be put into the project in the form of equity and how much you will get repaid to the investors. In Chapter 11 Structure a Deal, we will determine how to structure a deal (an investment) that might be appealing to third-party investors. But first, we need to create formats that a banker might like. We call those financial statements.

My theory has always been that financial statements are summaries of all the individual transactions that a business owner makes. They do tell stories, but they tell stories of what has happened. Let's now turn the tables, and create financial statements that tell us what may happen.

Creating Financial Statements

10

Financial statements provide summary information about how your business is working on a daily basis. Used to their full extent, they are the tools needed to propel the company forward and increase its value.

There are three basic types of financial statements:

■ Balance sheet—shows what a company has, what it owes, and what is left for the owner(s)

■ Income statement—tells how much a company is making, profitability

■ Cash flow statement—tells where money comes from and where it goes

These three financial statements are the tools used to manage the financial side of your business, and, as such, are part of the larger process of financial management. To understand how financial statements work, it is necessary to view them within the larger context of financial management.

The purpose of the three types of financial statements is to provide your business with a continuous source of data that can be used to:

■ Monitor cash flow

■ Analyze patterns and practices with the data, and

■ Ultimately to make the adjustments necessary to ensure a strong flow.

The balance sheet and income statement account for much of the information that makes up the financial statement. But not all of the sources of cash are income (i.e., cash that can be raised through investors or debt), and not all the uses of cash are expenses (i.e., they can be asset purchases or investments.)

Generating Numbers for Financial Statements

Financial statements are nothing more than a summary of each business decision or transaction that occurs in your business. The cash flow projections we have created thus far show where money came from and went to. But investors, especially bankers, will want to see your projected financial statements. So, we need to calculate some additional numbers on the *Projection* sheet so they can be summarized on the balance sheet and income statement.

Open file Chapter 10_Creating Financial Statements at www.nahb.org/financial forecasting and click on the *Projection* sheet. Figure 10.1 shows a partial view of lines 41 through 56. These calculations are not part of the projection itself, but will be needed to create the income statement, balance sheet, and cash flow statement as described later in this chapter.

Figure 10.1 Summarizing transactions to populate the balance sheet and income statement

	A	B	C	D	E	F	G	H
4	Period	1	2	3	4	5	6	7
6	Month	Jun-14	Jul-14	Aug-14	Sep-14	Oct-14	Nov-14	Dec-14
41	Outstanding loan balance:	0	33,750	168,750	427,500	798,750	1,046,250	1,068,750
42								
43	Sales	0	0	0	0	0	300000	600000
44	Collections	0	0	0	0	0	300,000	600,000
45		--------	--------	--------	--------	--------	--------	--------
46	A/R	0	0	0	0	0	0	0
47								
48	Purchases	7,500	86,250	292,500	356,250	513,750	525,000	435,000
49	COGS	0	0	0	0	0	-237,500	-475,000
50		--------	--------	--------	--------	--------	--------	--------
51	Ending Inventory	7,500	93,750	386,250	742,500	1,256,250	1,543,750	1,503,750
52								
53	Deposits	0	0	0	9,000	27,000	36,000	45,000
54								
55	Cumm. Capital contributions	800,000	800,000	800,000	800,000	800,000	800,000	800,000
56	Capital Distributions	0	0	0	0	0	-126,000	-282,600

On line 41, we determined the outstanding loan balance. This will show up on the balance sheet in the liability section.

Next we need to determine sales for the income statement and accounts receivable for the balance sheet. In order to create a running total, we need three lines: Sales, Collections, and Accounts Receivable (A/R). Sales is just current month sales times the average sales price: **=B8*Assumptions!$B$8**. Collections is the sum of cash collections and payments on accounts receivable or: **=SUM(B14:B15)**. The balance of accounts receivable is equal to last month's balance plus this month's sales minus this month's collections. The formula in cell C46 would look like this: **=B46+C43-C44**. The formula in cell B46 would not make reference to a previous month.

The next set of related numbers would be Inventory (on the balance sheet), Purchases, and Cost of Goods Sold (COGS). (Accounts Payable is also related to this concept, but because we borrow or finance our purchases, we can ignore this for now.) On lines B32 through B24, money is being expended for land deposits (a cost of construction, direct construction costs, and indirect construction costs). So, purchases or inventory are: =SUM(B21:B23). We relieve inventory through COGS. The real cost per unit is the sum of everything spent in these three categories divided by the number of units constructed. The formula is:

$$=-B8*SUM(\$N\$21:\$N\$23)/Assumptions!\$B\$7.$$

It starts with a negative as we subtract COGS from inventory. B8 is the sales for the month and the SUM($N$21:$N$24) is the total cost of all construction divided by the number of total units on the *Assumptions* page in cell B7.

Deposits, on line 53, are the previous month's deposits plus or minus the amount on line 16: =+B53+C16. (See Chapter 7, Deposits, Loans, Accounts Receivable, page 59 for further explanation.)

Populating the Balance Sheet and Income Statement

Here's a little more theory and then we'll apply this to the financial statements. Figure 10.2 shows lines 63–68 of the *Projection* sheet:

Figure 10.2 Finding balances based on a specific date or time frame

	A	B	C	D
4	Period	1	2	3
6	Month	Jun-14	Jul-14	Aug-14
7	Year	2014	2014	2014
62				
63		12/31/14	12/31/15	12/31/16
64	Financing Costs	94,500	67,500	0
65	Financing Costs with offset	94,500	67,500	0
66	Loan Balance	1,068,750	0	0
67	Loan Balance - with offset	1,068,750	0	0
68	Loan Balance - with offset	1,068,750	0	0

Figure 10.2 shows the results of various formulas which we will develop below. The first question—how much did we spend in each year for financing costs—will be used to populate the income statement. The second question—what was our loan balance at the end of each year of our projection—will populate the balance sheet.

For simplicity, we'll create the formulas for the income statement and balance sheet on the *Projection* worksheet and then bring them over to the pages for the balance sheet and income statement and allow Excel to create the worksheet references.

DATE and YEAR Functions

On line 7 of the *Projection* sheet, we need to create the year for each of the periods. This will be used in the search formulas on the financial statements. Enter this formula in B7: **=YEAR(B6)**. **Copy** this formula from B7 to C7 to M7.

On line 63 in cell B63, enter the formula: **=DATE(YEAR(Assumptions! $B$5),12,31)**. Assumptions!$B$5 is the date our projection begins (remember our beginning date is June 1, 2014). YEAR includes the year, which is 2014. Enter the month as 12 and the day as 31. It will return December 31, 2014. The date is important because a balance sheet is as of the end of a year (assuming a calendar year).

In cell C63, enter the formula: **=DATE(YEAR(B63)+1,12,31)** which adds one year to cell B63. **Copy** that formula to D63.

Income Statement Inputs

The income statement focuses on a period of time and makes use of the SUMIF statement. (See Chapter 9 Equity Needs, page 77 for the full discussion of SUMIF.) In this case, we will use the sum_range from the syntax:

=SUMIF(range, criteria, [sum_range]).

Assume you want to summarize financing costs by year. Our current projection covers two calendar years. The SUMIF function adds up the data in selected cells (line 24) when specific criteria are met (the year which we put in cell B63—2014) equals the year on line 7:

=SUMIF($B$7:$M$7,YEAR(B$63),$B$24:$M$24).

In this case, M7 is the last active month. Recall that column N contains the totals. But what happens if you add more columns to accommodate a longer projection period? You would need to rewrite formulas. Once again, this problem is solved by using the OFFSET formula. The objective is to add all columns before the total column.

The new formula would substitute the ending range parameter with an OFF-SET of the total column by "-1". The new formula (in cell B65) would be:

=SUMIF($B$7:OFFSET($N$7,0,-1),YEAR(B$63),$B$24:OFFSET($N$24,0,-1)).

If you added a new column N to accommodate period thirteen, the total column would be in column O. The formula would automatically adjust to:

=SUMIF($B$7:OFFSET($O$7,0,-1),YEAR(B$63),$B$24:OFFSET($O$24,0,-1)).

Again, as you make changes to your projection, you want the formulas to automatically adjust thereby saving you time and the potential for error. You can see both formulas on lines 64 and 65 of the *Projection* sheet.

The Balance Sheet Inputs

The balance sheet shows a value a particular point in time (e.g., year end) versus the income statement, which shows the activity during a period of time. This is confusing not only for non-accountants but many accountants as well. The balance sheet shows a balance, and the income statement shows activity.

HLOOKUP

In our spreadsheet we will use the HLOOKUP function. It tells Excel what value to search for from a list you designate, then returns the value in the same column offset by an index number. The syntax is:

=HLOOKUP(value, table_array, index_number, [not_exact_match])

The value is the value to search for in the first column of the table_array (for instance a date). The table_array is two or more columns of data that is sorted in ascending order. The index_number is a number of rows from the top of the table from which the matching value must be returned. The first column is 1. So if you want the value in row 2, you would enter 2. The not_exact_match is optional. It determines if you are looking for an exact match based on the value. Enter FALSE to find an exact match. Enter TRUE to find an approximate match.

Note:

- The index number can't be less than 1. If it is you will see "#VALUE!"

- If index_number is greater than the number of rows in the table_array, you will see #REF!

- If you specify FALSE for the not_exact_match parameter and no exact match is found, then you will see "#N/A".

The VLOOKUP function isn't used in this projection, but you may find it helpful in your work. It is similar to HLOOKUP except that it looks at the values on the left side of a table versus the side of a table. Everything else is identical. The syntax is:

=VLOOKUP(value, table_array, index_number, [not_exact_match])

All the definitions of the parameters are the same, except that the index number refers to the column number within the table array. For example, an index number of 2 would yield the value in the second column of the table (the first column with the values you are looking up is in column 1).

One last command is the LOOKUP command which is a remnant of older versions of Excel. Please don't use it as this function cannot be forced to find an exact match. It will pick the largest value that is less than or equal to the value you are looking up. This may cause errors in your calculations.

On the *Projection* sheet, suppose you want to find the loan balance as of December 31, 2014. The dates are on line 7. Recall that the dates display only month and year, but the formula is an end-of-month formula. So the value in the cell is the last day of the month (what you see is not the actual value). You can see the full value of the date by highlighting cell B6:M6 and formatting it to show the whole date (fig 10.3).

Figure 10.3 Formatting a cell to show a date

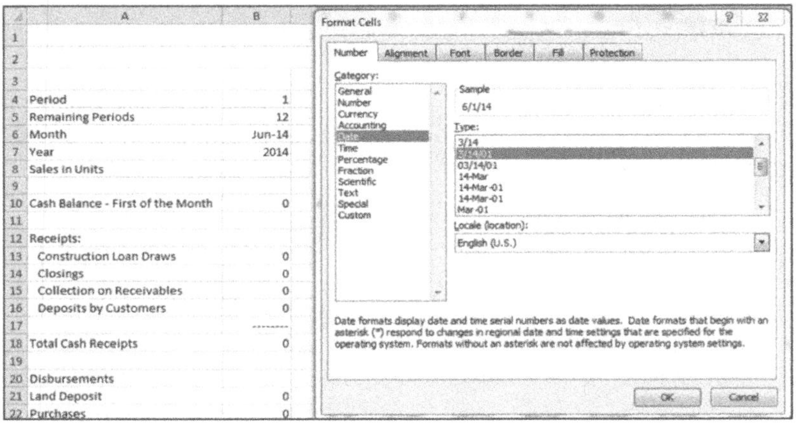

To calculate the balance of the loan on December 31, 2014, we want to look up that date in the ascending values on line 7 and then place the corresponding value on line 41. To do this we need an exact match; to define the table range; and to know the index number. Start with the simple setup in cell B67:

=HLOOKUP(B$63,$B$6:$N$44,36,FALSE).

This tells Excel to look up the date in cell B63 (which is 12/31/2014) in the table range B6:N44. The table must include the row from which we want the data. And include the value in the 36th row of our table (row 41 minus row 6 is 35 but we need to add one since the first row is row number 1 in the table). Finally, we want an exact match, so FALSE is added as the last argument.

But, figure 10.4 shows what happened in row C58: there is a "#N/A". This appears because the projection doesn't go out to 12/31/2015. How can we handle that?

Figure 10.4 Looking up a value that isn't in the table array

	A	B	C
65	Financing Costs with offset	94,500	67,500
66	Loan Balance	1,068,750	#N/A

IFERROR function

You can avoid having error messages appear in your worksheets by using the IFERROR function. It tells Excel that if a formula calculates to an error, it should populate the cell with a value you select instead of any of Excel's default error messages (e.g., #N/A, #VALUE!, #REF, etc.) Otherwise, it returns the result of the formula. This is known as *error trapping*. The syntax is: **=IFERROR(value, value_if_error).**

Value is a value or formula that is checked for the error. Value_if_error is the value you want in the cell in case of an error and it can be either a number or text. If it is text, the text needs to be in quotation marks.

In our spreadsheet, if we get an error, we want the formula to return the number zero ("0"). Thus we will amend our formula in cell C66 as follows:

=IFERROR(HLOOKUP(C$63,$B$6:$N$44,36,FALSE),0)

Figure 10.5 shows that with the IFERROR included in the function, we don't get an error.

Figure 10.5 Results of formula using the IFERROR function

	A	B	C	D
63		12/31/14	12/31/15	12/31/16
66	Loan Balance	1,068,750	0	0

Thinking ahead, we may want the index number to be calculated. This will help eliminate errors if we insert new rows or we want to reference different items (i.e., change the formula from finding an outstanding loan balance to finding the outstanding deposits). We want to be able to edit the row number without having to recalculate the number of rows from the table headings to the data we want.

ROW Function

The ROW function returns the row number of a cell reference. The syntax is =ROW([Reference]). The reference is the cell whose row number you want. For instance, =ROW(B5) would return 5.

Now, our formula in cell B67 would be:

$$=IFERROR(HLOOKUP(B\$63,\$B\$6:\$M\$44,$$
$$ROW(\$B\$41)-ROW(\$B\$6)+1,FALSE),0).$$

As we copy this formula from one cell to another, we can adjust the row number. This will save a lot of time when you insert rows. For instance, if we insert a new row 23 into our table on the *Projection* sheet, the formula would automatically adjust to:

$$=IFERROR(HLOOKUP(B\$63\$B\$6:\$M\$45,$$
$$ROW(\$B\$42)-ROW(\$B\$6)+1,FALSE),0).$$

Note: The ROW($B$41) adjusted to ROW($B$42).

That took care of the ROW problem, but what if you insert a column? The formulas that total a row's activity in column N might yield incorrect results. Again the OFFSET command is perfect. Instead of looking up our value in the tab B6:N44, we would make an OFFSET reference to N44 as follows:

$$=IFERROR(HLOOKUP(B\$55,\$B\$6:OFFSET(\$N\$44,0,-1),$$
$$ROW(\$B\$41)-ROW(\$B\$6)+1,FALSE),0).$$

Now if we insert another column (say column N) then the formula automatically adjusts to:

$$=IFERROR(HLOOKUP(B\$55,\$B\$6:OFFSET(\$O\$44,0,-1),$$
$$ROW(\$B\$41)-ROW(\$B\$6)+1,FALSE),0).$$

COLUMN Function

The COLUMN function returns the column number of a cell reference. The syntax is =COLUMN([Reference]). The reference is the cell whose column number you want. For instance, =COLUMN(C1) would return 3, as C is the third column on a spreadsheet.

We may want to get a column letter so we can reference the column letter. (We will discuss this in depth in Chapter 15 Advanced Concepts). The formula to convert column 3 to a letter C would be:

$$=CHAR(64+COLUMN()).$$

ADDRESS Function

The ADDRESS function is used to get the address of a cell in a worksheet, given specified row and column numbers. The syntax is:

$$=ADDRESS(row\_number, column\_number, abs\_num).$$

Simply put, **=Address(1,3)** would return $C$1. Note the absolute reference. The first two parameters are required: the row_number, a numeric value that specifies the row number, and the column_number, which, as you might guess, is the column number. The abs_num is optional, but if you put in a parameter it will return the appropriate reference.

- If you omit the third parameter or put a 1, you will get an absolute reference: **=ADDRESS(1,3,1)** returns $C$1.

- If the third parameter is 2, you will get an absolute row reference and a relative column reference: **=ADDRESS(1,3,2)** returns C$1.

- If the third parameter is 3, you will get a relative row reference and an absolute column reference: **=ADDRESS(1,3,3)** returns $C1.

- If the third parameter is 4, you will get a relative row and column reference: **=ADDRESS(1,3,4)** returns C1.

The Income Statement

Now that we have calculated all the numbers that we will need, we can create the financial statements. First is the income statement. There are three characteristics of an income statement, sometimes called a profit and loss (P & L) statement.

- It shows how much money a company is making or losing over a given time period.

- Despite its utility, an income statement alone cannot tell a reader whether a company is generally building or destroying wealth.

- An income statement is organized in "steps" that highlight key financial points for a company.

To read and understand an income statement, it is first necessary to understand the basic terminology.

- Net sales—the gross sales minus sales returns, sales allowances, and sales discounts

- Cost of goods sold—the net cost of bringing goods to market during the period covered by the statement. It tracks the flow of inventory and inventory-related costs in and out of a business.

- Gross profit—tells us how much is available to pay you and cover the costs of keeping your doors open

- Gross margin—this is a percentage of gross profit divided by gross sales

- Operating expenses—all expenses related to the sale of merchandise or services (selling expenses) plus all other costs related to operating the business (general and administrative expenses)

- Net income/net loss—generated when revenues exceed expenses, or conversely, when expenses exceed revenues

The next three terms are worth mentioning if you see them on your profit and loss:

- Non-operating income/non-operating expenses—the results of activities other than those for which the business was originally organized, such as interest, income, or rent. They can either be included on an income statement separately, or as part of the other revenue and expenses.

- Extraordinary gains/losses—significant or material gains or losses resulting from events that are *both* unusual in nature (not expected to be frequent) and infrequent in occurrence (unrelated to daily operations), including casualty losses, debt, and capital restructuring. Extraordinary gains and losses are shown net of tax effects.

- Non-recurring items—material gains or losses resulting from events that are either unusual in nature or infrequent in occurrence, such as the sale of property or other operating assets.

Figure 10.6 shows a sample income statement.

Figure 10.6 A sample income statement

```
                    SAMPLE COMPANY
                    INCOME STATEMENT
                YEAR ENDED DECEMBER 31, 200_

Revenue from Sales
  Sales                                      $98,010
    Sales Returns and Allowances    $2,954
    Sales Discounts                 $1,056   $4,010
  Net Sales                                           $94,000

Cost of Goods Sold
  Beginning inventory                        $30,210
  Purchases                         $45,390
    Purchase Discounts              $3,180
    Net Purchases                   $42,210
    Transportation                  $1,780
    Delivered Cost of Purchase               $43,990
  Cost of Goods Available for Sale           $74,200
  Ending Inventory                          ($32,150)
  Cost of Goods Sold                                  $42,050
Gross Profit on Sales                                 $51,950

Operating Expenses
  Selling
    Sales Commisions                $14,390
    Advertising                     $2,130
    Delivery                        $1,200
    Supplies                        $1,230
    Bad Debt Expense                $1,500
    Total Selling Expenses                   $20,450

  Administrative
    Office Salaries                 $11,365
    Business Taxes                  $1,500
    Depreciation                    $13,635
    Utilities                       $1,750
    Sundry Office Expenses          $250
    Total Administrative Expenses            $28,500
  Total Operating Expenses                            $48,950

Net income from Operations                            $3,000

Other Income
  Extraordinary Gain on Sale of Equipment             $3,000

Net Income                                            $6,000
```

An income statement, like a balance sheet, can be compared to industry-wide averages for similar data and serves multiple purposes. It enables you to answer these questions:

- Are revenues where I want them?
- Am I controlling my variable costs?
- Am I pricing my products correctly (gross margin)?
- Am I selling the right products?
- Are my costs of running the business in line?
- Am I profitable?

Historical income statements serve as a guide to potential lenders and/or investors by providing an indication of past performance, which is often seen as an indicator of future performance. The projection is an indication of future performance.

Creating an Income Statement

The file Chapter 10_Creating Financial Statements found at www.nahb.org/financial forecasting includes an *Income Statement* sheet. The income statement is already set up, but we have included the detailed instructions here if you want to recreate this on your own.

1) Set up the headings.

- Create a new worksheet and title the tab *Income Statement.*
- In cell A1, type: **=Assumptions!A1.**
- On line 2, type *Projected Income Statement.*
- On line 3, type *Prepared by: Management* (or whomever).
- Line 4, type *For the Year(s) Ended December 31.*
- Highlight the range A1:F6, **right click** and choose format cells, go to the **Alignment** tab and under horizontal, choose "Center Across Selection" and then click **OK.**
- On line B6, enter *Year* then align that over the columns B through F. Put an outside border around those cells.
- Finally, if you want to show totals for the years of the projections, add the word *Total* in cell G6 and put an outside border around that cell.

2) Put in the years.

- Go to cell B7 and enter: **=YEAR(Assumptions!$B$5).** This returns the year of the beginning date.
- Go to cell C7 and enter: **=+B7+1.** This increments the year by one.
- **Copy** C7 to column F.

3) Set up your row headings as shown in figure 10.7.

- We'll use a simple income statement structure, but you can make this as formal as you like.

Figure 10.7 Row descriptions for the income statement

	A
9	Revenue
10	
11	Sales
12	Less: Cost of Goods Sold
13	
14	Gross Profit
15	Gross Profit Percent
16	
17	Overhead Expenses
18	Financing Costs (Interest)
19	Marketing Costs
20	General & Administrative Costs
21	
22	Total Overhead Expenses
23	
24	Net Income Before Taxes
25	Net Income Percent

4) Format the spreadsheet with totals and subtotals (fig 10.8).

Figure 10.8 Setting up the income statement skeleton

	A	B	C	D	E	F	G
9	Revenue						
10							
11	Sales	0	0	0	0	0	0
12	Less: Cost of Goods Sold	0	0	0	0	0	0
13							
14	Gross Profit	0	0	0	0	0	0
15	Gross Profit Percent	0%	0%	0%	0%	0%	
16							
17	Overhead Expenses						
18	Financing Costs (Interest)	0	0	0	0	0	0
19	Marketing Costs	0	0	0	0	0	0
20	General & Administrative Costs	0	0	0	0	0	0
21							
22	Total Overhead Expenses	0	0	0	0	0	0
23							
24	Net Income Before Taxes	0	0	0	0	0	0
25	Net Income Percent	0%	0%	0%	0%	0%	

- We use SUM formulas in rows 14 and 22.
- In row 24, add row 14 minus row 22: **=B14-B22**.
- In row 15, compute gross profit percent: **=IF(B11=0,0,B14/B11)**. The IF statement is used to error trap. It says that if B11 =0 use 0 (otherwise if B11 equals zero a "#DIV/" error would appear). We could have used: **=IFERROR(B14/B11,0)** and get the same results. IFERROR is a more recent addition to the Excel functions.
- Column G is the sum of columns B:F.

The formulas are shown in figure 10.9.

Figure 10.9 The formulas for the income statement skeleton

	A	B	C	D	E	F	G
9	Revenue						
10							
11	Sales						=SUM(B11:F11)
12	Less: Cost of Goods Sold						=SUM(B12:F12)
13		———	———	———	———	———	
14	Gross Profit	=SUM(B11:B13)	=SUM(C11:C13)	=SUM(D11:D13)	=SUM(E11:E13)	=SUM(F11:F13)	=SUM(G11:G13)
15	Gross Profit Percent	=IF(B11=0,0,B14/B11)	=IF(C11=0,0,C14/C11)	=IF(D11=0,0,D14/D11)	=IF(E11=0,0,E14/E11)	=IF(F11=0,0,F14/F11)	
16							
17	Overhead Expenses						
18	=+Projection!A24						=SUM(B18:F18)
19	=+Projection!A25						=SUM(B19:F19)
20	=+Projection!A26						=SUM(B20:F20)
21		———	———	———	———	———	
22	Total Overhead Expenses	=SUM(B18:B21)	=SUM(C17:C21)	=SUM(D17:D21)	=SUM(E17:E21)	=SUM(F17:F21)	=SUM(B22:F22)
23		———	———	———	———	———	
24	Net Income Before Taxes	=+B14-B22	=+C14-C22	=+D14-D22	=+E14-E22	=+F14-F22	=SUM(B24:F24)
25	Net Income Percent	=IFERROR(+B24/B11,0)	=IFERROR(+C24/C11,0)	=IFERROR(+D24/D11,0)	=IFERROR(+E24/E11,0)	=IFERROR(+F24/F11,0)	

5) Create links to your *Projection* worksheet.

■ Recall our financing formula in cell B65 on our *Projection* sheet:

=SUMIF($B$7:OFFSET($N$7,0,-1),YEAR(B$63),$B$24:OFFSET($N$24,0,-1))

■ Now we have to amend it because it is on a new sheet:

**=SUMIF(Projection!$B$7:OFFSET(Projection!$N$7,0,-1),B$7,
Projection!$B$24:OFFSET(Projection!$N$24,0,-1))**

■ The formulas are essentially the same, but because we are referencing another sheet, we need to identify that sheet "Projection!" and we change our year reference to B$7, which is already converted into a year.

■ It would be nice just to copy this formula from one line to another, but the reference to $B$24:OFFSET(Projection!$N$24,0,-1) keeps changing depending on what you want to bring over. You can use a shortcut: In column I (fig 10.10), enter: **=ROW(Projection!B24)** to get the pertinent row number. Then edit the formulas to the appropriate row number as indicated in column I. Note: Once you make a reference, if you add or delete lines, formulas adjust automatically, which is the beauty of this system.

Figure 10.10 The projected income statement populated

	A	B	C	D	E	F	G	H	I
2				Projected Income Statement					
3				Prepared by: Management					
4				For the Year(s) Ended December 31,					
5									
6					Year		Total		
7			2014	2015	2016	2017	2018		
8									
9	Revenue								Row
10									Number
11	Sales	900,000	2,700,000	0	0	0	3,600,000		43
12	Less: Cost of Goods Sold	-712,500	-2,137,500	0	0	0	-2,850,000		49
13		-------	-------	-------	-------	-------	-------		
14	Gross Profit	187,500	562,500	0	0	0	750,000		
15	Gross Profit Percent	21%	21%	0%	0%	0%			
16									
17	Overhead Expenses								
18	Financing Costs (Interest)	94,500	67,500	0	0	0	162,000		24
19	Marketing Costs	86,400	57,600	0	0	0	144,000		25
20	General & Administrative Costs	84,000	60,000	0	0	0	144,000		26
21		-------	-------	-------	-------	-------	-------		
22	Total Overhead Expenses	264,900	185,100	0	0	0	450,000		
23		-------	-------	-------	-------	-------	-------		
24	Net Income Before Taxes	-77,400	377,400	0	0	0	300,000		
25	Net Income Percent	-9%	14%	0%	0%	0%			

Figure 10.11 shows the formulas (for sake of space we will only show columns A through B):

Figure 10.11 A partial view of the income statement formulas

	A	B
11	Sales	=SUMIF(Projection!$B$7:OFFSET(Projection!$N$7,0,-1),B$7,Projection!$B$43:OFFSET(Projection!$N$43,0,-1))
12	Less: Cost of Goods Sold	=SUMIF(Projection!$B$7:OFFSET(Projection!$N$7,0,-1),B$7,Projection!$B$49:OFFSET(Projection!$N$49,0,-1))
13		
14	Gross Profit	=SUM(B11:B13)
15	Gross Profit Percent	=IF(B11=0,0,B14/B11)
16		
17	Overhead Expenses	
18	=+Projection!A24	=SUMIF(Projection!$B$7:OFFSET(Projection!$N$7,0,-1),B$7,Projection!$B$24:OFFSET(Projection!$N$24,0,-1))
19	=+Projection!A25	=SUMIF(Projection!$B$7:OFFSET(Projection!$N$7,0,-1),B$7,Projection!$B$25:OFFSET(Projection!$N$25,0,-1))
20	=+Projection!A26	=SUMIF(Projection!$B$7:OFFSET(Projection!$N$7,0,-1),B$7,Projection!$B$26:OFFSET(Projection!$N$26,0,-1))
21		
22	Total Overhead Expenses	=SUM(B16:B21)
23		
24	Net Income Before Taxes	=+B14-B22
25	Net Income Percent	=IFERROR(+B24/B11,0)

Yes, this is complicated, but if you study and play with the formulas on lines 18 through 20, it will eventually begin to make more sense.

The Balance Sheet

A balance sheet is a snapshot of a company's financial status at a given moment in time—typically at the end of a financial period (though they can also be monthly, quarterly, or on demand). A balance sheet is created from three types of information: *assets, liability,* and *equity.*

To understand a balance sheet, think of buying a new car. You need a loan. The bank manager asks you to give the bank a picture of your financial situation. So, you take a sheet of paper, divide it into two, and put everything you own (e.g., your house, car(s), investments, etc.) and the corresponding values on the left side and everything you owe (e.g., mortgage, car loans, etc), with the corresponding values on the right side. The difference between the total amounts of the two sides is your net wealth. Similarly, a corporate balance sheet is a statement of a company's net wealth.

Like the sheet of paper you showed to the bank manager, a balance sheet is often presented in a two-column format (fig 10.12).

Figure 10.12 The balance sheet structure illustrating assets = liabilities + equity

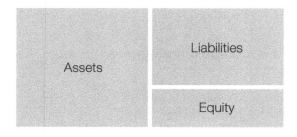

The asset column is always on the left (fig 10.13) and the liabilities and equity are always on the right (fig 10.14).

Figure 10.13 The left-hand column of the balance sheet shows the assets.

```
                     SAMPLE COMPANY
                     BALANCE SHEET
                   DECEMBER 31, 200X
```

	Full Accrual	
	Amount	Percent
Current Assets		
Cash	$21,500	12%
Accounts Receivable	$28,950	16%
Inventory	$32,150	18%
Supplies	$1,100	1%
Total Current Assets	$83,700	47%
Fixed Assets		
Land	$15,500	9%
Building	$100,000	56%
Equipment	$95,000	53%
Acc. Dep	($140,445)	-78%
Total Fixed Assets	$70,055	39%
Intangible Assets		
Goodwill	$25,500	14%
Total Intangible Assets	$25,500	14%
Total Assets	$179,255	100%

Figure 10.14 The right-hand column of the balance sheet shows liabilities and equity.

```
                     SAMPLE COMPANY
                     BALANCE SHEET
                   DECEMBER 31, 200X
```

	Amount	Percent
Liabilities		
Current Liabilities		
Accounts Payable	$21,940	12%
Salaries Payable	$2,310	1%
Taxes Payable	$1,250	1%
Total Current Liabilities	$25,500	14%
Noncurrent Liabilities		
Long Term Debt	$70,500	39%
Total Liabilities	$96,000	54%
Owners' Equity		
Common Shares	$50,000	28%
Retained Earnings	$33,255	19%
Total Owners' Equity	$83,255	46%
Total Liabilities & Owners' Equity	$179,255	100%

In order to balance as a balance sheet must, the total assets must equal the total liabilities plus equity. Mathematically, this represents a fundamental equation of accounting:

$$\text{Assets} = \text{Liabilities} + \text{Equity}$$

Before creating a balance sheet, it is important to understand the definitions of each of the three components.

Assets

Assets are economic resources that are expected to produce economic benefits for their owner. They can be buildings, machinery, patents, copyrights, or even money owed to the firm by customers. Assets fall within two categories:

- Current—Assets that will be transformed into cash or used within one year, or the normal operating cycle if more than one year. (e.g., cash, marketable securities, accounts receivable, inventories, and pre-paid expenses.)

- Non-current/long-term—Assets that will not be consumed within one year, or the normal operating cycle. (i.e., tangible items such as property, the plant, and equipment, and intangible items such as patents, copyrights, and goodwill.)

The rationale for having two types of assets is to highlight liquidity and thus assist in predicting cash flow.

Liabilities

Liabilities are obligations a company owes to outside parties. They represent the rights of others to money or services from the company. Typical examples are bank loans and debts to suppliers or employees. Like assets, there are two categories of liabilities:

- Current—Claims against a company that will be satisfied within a year or the normal operating cycle. (e.g., accounts payable, wages payable, accrued expenses, taxes payable, and the current portion of notes payable.)

- Non-current/long-term—Liabilities that are outstanding for more than a year or the normal operating cycle. (e.g., mortgages, bonds payable, and long-term notes.) Keep in mind that non-current liabilities can be current at the same time if part of the liability must be satisfied within the current year or normal operating cycle.

Equity

The value of a business to its owners after all obligations have been met. This net worth (i.e., the difference between what it owns and what it owes) belongs to the owners, or is owner-invested capital. There are two broad classes of equity:

■ *Capital contributions* are funds from the owners of the company.

■ *Retained earnings* are any profits that are reinvested into the company.

The balance sheet must answer these questions:

• **Does the company have the proper level of fixed assets?** Fixed assets should not be so excessive so as to reduce a company's ability to continue operating.

• **Does the company have sufficient working capital to handle sales volume?** In other words, do you have the liquid assets necessary to handle inventory and accounts receivable as you grow?

• **Is the company solvent?** There should be enough assets to adequately cover all debt.

• **Can the company pay its bills?** There should be enough cash to cover all current expenses.

• **Is the company building wealth?** If the equity on the current balance sheet is compared to the equity on previous balance sheets, there should be an overall increase—thereby showing growth in wealth.

Creating a Balance Sheet with Your Projection

As with the income statement, the file Chapter 10_Creating Financial Statements found at www.nahb.org/financialforecasting also includes *Balance Sheet* page. The balance sheet is already set up, but we have included the detailed instructions here if you want to recreate this on your own.

1) Set up the headings

■ Create a new worksheet called *Balance Sheet*

■ In cell A1, type: **=Assumptions!A1**, which is the company name.

■ On Line 2, type *Projected Balance Sheet* as shown in figure 10.15.

■ On Line 3, type *Prepared by: Management* (or whomever).

■ Highlight the range A1:F5, **right click** and choose format cells, go to the **Alignment** tab and under horizontal, choose "Center Across Selection" and then click **OK.**

■ Line 4, type *Period Ended* in cell A5.

Figure 10.15 Headings for the projected balance sheet

	A	B	C	D	E	F
1		Sample Company				
2		Projected Balance Sheet				
3		Prepared by: Management				

2) Enter the years

■ In cell B5 enter: **=DATE(YEAR(Assumptions!$B$5),12,31)**. This will give us the first year end.

■ In cell C5, enter: **=DATE(YEAR(B5)+1,12,31)**, which will set up the next year. **Copy** that formula to F5 as shown in figure 10.16.

Figure 10.16 Creating the period end dates

	A	B	C	D	E	F
5	Period Ended	12/31/14	12/31/15	12/31/16	12/31/17	12/31/18

3) Set up your row headings as shown in figure 10.17

■ For Assets we'll use a simple structure—but you can make this as formal as you like.

Figure 10.17 Setting up the row descriptions for the assets

	A
6	Assets
7	Current Assets
8	Cash
9	Accounts Receivable
10	Inventory
11	Prepaid Expenses
12	Other Current Assets
13	
14	Total Current Assets
15	
16	Fixed Assets
17	Gross Fixed Assets
18	Accumulated Depreciation
19	
20	Net Fixed Assets
21	
22	Total Assets

Note: for purposes of the forecasted balance sheet we are going to put the "right hand" side of the balance sheet below the assets. We will test for equality (assets equal liabilities and equity) in step 7 of this section. The row headings for

Liabilities and Equity are shown in figure 10.18. Remember to create the equity section based on the type of entity—partnership, corporation, etc.

Figure 10.18 Setting up the row descriptions for the liabilities and equity

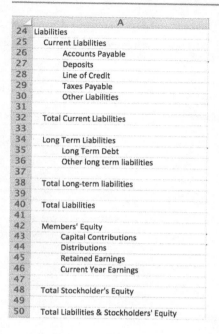

	A
24	Liabilities
25	Current Liabilities
26	Accounts Payable
27	Deposits
28	Line of Credit
29	Taxes Payable
30	Other Liabilities
31	
32	Total Current Liabilities
33	
34	Long Term Liabilities
35	Long Term Debt
36	Other long term liabilities
37	
38	Total Long-term liabilities
39	
40	Total Liabilities
41	
42	Members' Equity
43	Capital Contributions
44	Distributions
45	Retained Earnings
46	Current Year Earnings
47	
48	Total Stockholder's Equity
49	
50	Total Liabilities & Stockholders' Equity

4) Format the spreadsheet with totals and subtotals (create the skeleton)

■ The formulas for the Asset side are shown in figure 10.19.

Figure 10.19 The formulas for the asset section

	A	B	C	D	E	F
1	=Assumptions!$A$1					
2			Projected Balance Sheet			
3			Prepared by: Management			
4						
5	="Period Ended"	=DATE(YEAR(Assumptic	=DATE(YEAR(B5)+1,12	=DATE(YEAR(C5)+1,12,3	=DATE(YEAR(D5)+1,12	=DATE(YEAR(E5)+1,12,
6	Assets					
7	Current Assets					
8	Cash	=IFERROR(HLOOKUP(B$5	=IFERROR(HLOOKUP(C$	=IFERROR(HLOOKUP(D$5	=IFERROR(HLOOKUP(E$	=IFERROR(HLOOKUP(F$5
9	Accounts Receivable	=IFERROR(HLOOKUP(B$5	=IFERROR(HLOOKUP(C$	=IFERROR(HLOOKUP(D$5	=IFERROR(HLOOKUP(E$	=IFERROR(HLOOKUP(F$5
10	Inventory	=IFERROR(HLOOKUP(B$5	=IFERROR(HLOOKUP(C$	=IFERROR(HLOOKUP(D$5	=IFERROR(HLOOKUP(E$	=IFERROR(HLOOKUP(F$5
11	Prepaid Expenses	=IFERROR(HLOOKUP(B$5	=IFERROR(HLOOKUP(C$	=IFERROR(HLOOKUP(D$5	=IFERROR(HLOOKUP(E$	=IFERROR(HLOOKUP(F$5
12	Other Current Assets	=IFERROR(HLOOKUP(B$5	=IFERROR(HLOOKUP(C$	=IFERROR(HLOOKUP(D$5	=IFERROR(HLOOKUP(E$	=IFERROR(HLOOKUP(F$5
13		--------	--------	--------	--------	--------
14	Total Current Assets	=SUM(B8:B13)	=SUM(C8:C13)	=SUM(D8:D13)	=SUM(E8:E13)	=SUM(F8:F13)
15						
16	Fixed Assets					
17	Gross Fixed Assets	0	0	0	0	0
18	Accumulated Depreciation	0	0	0	0	0
19		--------	--------	--------	--------	--------
20	Net Fixed Assets	=SUM(B17:B19)	=SUM(C17:C19)	=SUM(D17:D19)	=SUM(E17:E19)	=SUM(F17:F19)
21		--------	--------	--------	--------	--------
22	Total Assets	=B14+B20	=C14+C20	=D14+D20	=E14+E20	=F14+F20

■ The formulas for the Liability and Equity side are shown in figure 10.20.

Figure 10.20 The formulas for the liabilities and equity section

	A	B	C	D	E	F
24	Liabilities					
25	Current Liabilities					
26	Accounts Payable	0	0	0	0	0
27	Deposits	=IFERROR(HLOOKUP(B$5	=IFERROR(HLOOKUP(C$	=IFERROR(HLOOKUP(D$5	=IFERROR(HLOOKUP(E$	=IFERROR(HLOOKUP(F$5
28	Line of Credit	0	0	0	0	0
29	Taxes Payable	0	0	0	0	0
30	Other Liabilities	0	0	0	0	0
31						
32	Total Current Liabilities	=SUM(B26:B31)	=SUM(C26:C31)	=SUM(D26:D31)	=SUM(E26:E31)	=SUM(F26:F31)
33						
34	Long Term Liabilities					
35	Long Term Debt	=IFERROR(HLOOKUP(B$5	=IFERROR(HLOOKUP(C$	=IFERROR(HLOOKUP(D$5	=IFERROR(HLOOKUP(E$	=IFERROR(HLOOKUP(F$5
36	Other long term liabilities	0	0	0	0	0
37						
38	Total Long-term liabilities	=SUM(B35:B37)	=SUM(C35:C37)	=SUM(D35:D37)	=SUM(E35:E37)	=SUM(F35:F37)
39						
40	Total Liabilities	=+B32+B38	=+C32+C38	=+D32+D38	=+E32+E38	=+F32+F38
41						
42	Members' Equity					
43	Capital Contributions	=SUMIF(Projection!$B$7	=SUMIF(Projection!B	=SUMIF(Projection!$B$7	=SUMIF(Projection!B	=SUMIF(Projection!$B$7
44	Distributions	=SUMIF(Projection!$B$7	=SUMIF(Projection!B	=SUMIF(Projection!$B$7	=SUMIF(Projection!B	=SUMIF(Projection!$B$7
45	Retained Earnings	0	=SUM(B45:B46)	=SUM(C45:C46)	=SUM(D45:D46)	=SUM(E45:E46)
46	Current Year Earnings	='Income Statement'!B24	='Income Statement'!C$	='Income Statement'!D24	='Income Statement'!E2	='Income Statement'!F2$
47						
48	Total Stockholder's Equity	=SUM(B43:B46)	=SUM(C43:C46)	=SUM(D43:D46)	=SUM(E43:E46)	=SUM(F43:F46)
49						
50	Total Liabilities & Stockholders' Equity	=+B40+B48	=+C40+C48	=+D40+D48	=+E40+E48	=+F40+F48

5) Create links to your *Projection* worksheet.

■ Recall our discussion on the ROW formulas on page 88:

$$=IFERROR(HLOOKUP(B\$63,\$B\$6:OFFSET(\$N\$44,0,-1),$$
$$ROW(\$B\$41)-ROW(\$B\$6)+1,FALSE),0).$$

■ I like to create a row reference in the part of the page that won't get printed out. For instance, ending cash is on line 37 of the *Projection* sheet. So in column H, put a formula **=ROW(Projection!B37)**, which leaves a number "37." This makes the next formula easier:

$$=IFERROR(HLOOKUP(B\$5,Projection!\$B\$6:OFFSET(Projection!$$
$$\$N\$56,0,-1),\$H8-ROW(Projection!\$B\$6)+1,FALSE),0).$$

This says to look in the projection whose range is defined as B6 to N56, get the BALANCE from the row in column H then subtract 6 (the row from ROW(Projection!$B$6) and add 1 to that *if* there is an exact match.

■ **Copy** this formula into all asset and liabilities with the exception of the equity section of the balance sheet.

6) The Equity section

The equity section is a little tricky. For the Capital Contributions and Distributions, we want a SUMIF statement similar to that on an income statement.

- For the contributions, year 1 would look like this:

=SUMIF(Projection!$B$7:OFFSET(Projection!$N$7,0,- 1),YEAR(B$5), Projection!$B$34:_ OFFSET(Projection!$N$34,0,-1)).

- For the contributions past year 1, we need to add prior year contributions as well:

=SUMIF(Projection!$B$7:OFFSET(Projection!$N$7,0,-1),YEAR(C$5), Projection!$B$34:OFFSET(Projection!$N$34,0,-1))+B43
(which adds in the prior year).

- For distributions, we have the exact same formulas except that N34 becomes N35.
- For retained earnings, in year 1 the retained earnings are zero as we have no former years to account for (if you have operations from prior years, then additional work is necessary, namely adding an historical balance sheet). For years two through the end of your projection period, the formula is: =SUM(B45:B46), which of course you **copy** from C45 to F45.
- Current year earning come from the income statement: ='Income Statement'!B24

7) The Proof: Control Totals

When working with tables that have totals on columns and rows I like to have a "control" total that cross checks to make sure the totals add up correctly. My control total should always come back to 0 to indicate there is no discrepancy.

- The assets must equal liabilities and equity. I add a statement to prove that they are in balance on line 52.
- The formula in cell B52 looks like this: **=IF(AND(B22-B50>-1,B22-B50<1)**, " ",B50-B22) which tells Excel if assets minus liabilities and equity are equal to zero then leave a blank cell, otherwise show the difference. The space with a quotation mark around it is leaves a null value in the cell.
- This is the most important formula in the whole spreadsheet. If these are out of balance you have a programming problem somewhere in the pro forma. Looking for blank cells is much easier than looking at numbers to see if they are in balance.

The Cash Flow Statement

Remember, a financial statement only summarizes what you've already done. Thus, almost all our information comes from our cash flow projections. In the cash flow statement, we are trying to determine where our cash is coming *from* and going *to*.

Cash can be generated through three sources:

■ Operating activities—Funds generated or used internally from the normal business activities of your firm.

■ Investing activities—Funds generated or used for the purchase of long-term assets that show up on the balance sheet, such as plant and equipment and investment activities.

■ Financing activities—Externally generated funds that impact long-term debt, such as the issuance or redemption of bonds or loans, and/or equity (i.e., the issuance or redemption of stock), as reflected on the balance sheet.

To understand the nature of cash flow, consider the fact that a business can survive without profit, but not without cash. This is true because profit is just one part of a larger financial picture. Cash is not generated or spent solely through the revenues and expenses shown on an income statement. As shown in the cash flow diagram on page 2, cash can also be generated via loans and capital infusions, and can be spent on assets such as intangibles, equipment, debt payments, and investments. The following simple example illustrates how a transaction that would simply be an expense on an income statement is actually a generator of cash when accounted for on a cash flow statement.

A company purchases a piece of equipment that costs $10,000, and takes out a $7,000 loan to do so. The company then has $3,000 of cash invested in the equipment:

Cost:	$10,000
Less:	$7,000 loan
Cash In:	$3,000

The company then sells the equipment for $9,000, $1,000 less than the cost (ignoring depreciation). The income statement would then show a loss:

Sales Price:	$9,000
Cost:	$10,000
Profit (Loss):	($1,000)

But, while the income statement only shows the profit and loss of the situation, the cash flow statement shows how much *cash* was actually generated or lost—in this case, $2,000 was generated:

Cash Received:	$9,000
Loan:	$7,000
Cash Generated:	$2,000

This example illustrates how an income statement or balance sheet alone is insufficient to provide a complete financial assessment of a company. The cash flow statement fills in the details that the other two statements leave out. A sample cash flow statement is shown in figure 10.21.

Figure 10.21 A sample cash flow statement

```
                    SAMPLE COMPANY
              STATEMENT OF CHANGES IN CASH
              YEAR ENDED DECEMBER 31,200_

Funds from Operation
Net Income                              $6,000
Add (subtract) items that did not invove a cash inflow or outflow:
Depreciation                           $13,365
                                                 $19,365

Decrease in Supplies                    $200
Increase in Inventories                 $3,000
Increase in Accounts Receivable        (5,790.00)
Decrease in Accounts Payable           (6,340.00)
Increase in Salaries Payable            1,200.00
Increase in Taxes Payable               550.00   (7,180.00)

Cash from Operations                             $12,185

Financing Activities
Increase in LT Debt                    10,000.00
Dividends                              (2,000.00)
Cash from Financing Activities                   $8,000

Investing Activities
Sale of Equipment                      10,000.00
Purchase of Equipment                  (9,300.00)
Cash from Investing Activities                   $700

Net Increases in Cash                            $20,885
Cash, beginning of Period                        $615

Cash, End of Period                              $21,500
```

Cash shortages, particularly during growth stages, are possible since the company is turning liquid assets (cash) into other types of assets such as inventory and accounts receivable, in order to support the growth. If the company is profitable, cash inflows will ultimately exceed cash outflows.

A cash flow statement should answer the following questions:

■ **Is money being generated through operations?** Cash flow generated by operations should be positive—indicating that the company is fulfilling its mission.

■ **Is money being reinvested in the company?** If investing cash flow is negative, it indicates that the company is buying assets faster than it is selling them. It is normal for start-ups and expanding companies to have a negative cash flow.

■ **Is money being generated through financing?** The answer to this question can be interpreted in different ways. For instance, a large amount of money coming in through financing might be an indicator that the company is expanding. Conversely, it could indicate that the company is desperate for cash and financing everything in sight.

Creating a Cash Flow Statement with Your Projection

As with the other financial statements, the file Chapter 10_Creating Financial Statements found at www.nahb.org/financialforecasting includes *Cash Flow Statement* sheet. The cash flow statement is already set up, but we have included the detailed instructions here if you want to recreate this on your own.

Before we get into the actual formulas, let's cover a little more theory. The balance sheet is a statement at a point in time; the income statement covers a period. So, if we want to see if cash is created or destroyed on our balance sheet, we need to look at the beginning balances versus the ending balances. Let's analyze accounts receivable in figure 10.22. Suppose we have no beginning balances and sales of $100,000 and ending accounts receivable of $10,000. How much cash did we generate?

Figure 10.22 Cash generated through sales

Beginning A/R	0.00
Plus: Sales	100,000.00
Less Ending A/R	10,000.00

Cash Received	90,000.00

As you can see, we only generated $90,000. But on the income statement we would have sales of $100,000. So, if we look at income, we need to adjust it by the difference between ending accounts receivable and beginning. If receivables go up, then we are losing cash (because people owe it to us and we have not collected it yet) and if receivables are going down (i.e., we were owed $10,000 at the beginning of the year and at the end of the year we were owed $5,000, then we collected a net $5,000 during the year).

All asset balances work this way. Thus, if you subtract ending balance from beginning balance and the number is positive, you created cash, and if it is negative, you used cash. Liabilities work just the opposite. If your liabilities go up, then you aren't paying someone. As an example, let's analyze accounts payable. In figure 10.23 we have no beginning balance and purchase of $80,000 and ending accounts payable of $5,000. How much cash did we spend (liabilities ultimately must be paid)? (This is the same question as accounts receivable.)

Figure 10.23 Cash spent on purchases

Beginning A/P	0.00
Plus: Purchases	80,000.00
Less: Ending A/P	5,000.00

Cash Spent	75,000.00

As you can see, our purchases were $80,000 but we spent $75,000. And if payables (a liability) increase, then we are saving cash (because we got stuff but haven't paid for it yet). And, if payables are decreasing, then we are disbursing cash with no corresponding purchase.

All liability balances work this way. But in this case, if you subtract beginning balances from ending balances and the number is positive you created cash, and if it negative, you used cash. The exact opposite of asset balances!

The trick is to understand the difference between an asset and a liability, which is easy because we look on the balance sheet and see where it is. We have the same steps as the income statement or balance sheet, but the formulas change.

1): Set up the headings.

■ Create a new worksheet called *Cash Flow Statement.*

■ In cell A1, type: **=Assumptions!A1**, which is the company name.

■ On Line 2, type *Statement of Cash Flows.*

■ On Line 3, type *Prepared by: Management (*or whomever).

■ Highlight rows A1 to F5, **right click** and choose format cells, go to the **Alignment** tab and under horizontal, choose "Center Across Selection" and then click **OK.**

■ Line 4, type *Period Ended* in cell A5.

2) Enter the years.

■ In cell B5, enter: **=YEAR(Assumptions!$B$5)**. This will give us the first year end.

■ In cell C5, enter: **=+B5+1**, which will set up the next year. **Copy** that formula to F5.

3) Enter your row headings as shown in figure 10.24.

Figure 10.24 Row descriptions for the cash flow statement

	A
6	Operating Activities
7	Net Income (loss)
8	Adjusments to reconcile net income
9	to net cash used by operating activities:
10	Depreciation
11	Amortization
12	Changes in operating assets & liabiities
13	Accounts Receivable
14	Inventory
15	Prepaid Expenses
16	Other Current Assets
17	Accounts Payable
18	Deposits
19	Line of Credit
20	Taxes Payable
21	Other Liabilities
22	
23	Total Cash used in operating activities
24	
25	Investing Activities:
26	Net Increase/Decrease in Investment Assets
27	Net Property & Equipment Activity
28	Purchase of Intangible Assets
29	
30	Net Cash used in Investing Activities:
31	
32	Financing Activities
33	Net Proceeds from Notes Payable
34	Net Proceeds from Other Long Term Liabilities
35	Proceeds from the issuance of Stock
36	Dividends
37	
38	Net Cash Used in Financing Activities
39	
40	Net Increase (Decrease) in Cash
41	
42	*Proof*
43	Ending Cash
44	Beginning Cash
45	
46	Net Increase (Decrease) in Cash

4) Format the spreadsheet with totals and subtotals as shown in figure 10.25

Figure 10.25 Formulas for the skeleton of the cash flow statement

	A	B	C	D	E	F
6	Operating Activities					
7	Net Income (loss)	=+'Income Statement'!B24	=+'Income Statement'!C2	=+'Income Statement'!D2	=+'Income Statement'!E2	=+'Income Statement'!F2
8	Adjusments to reconcile net income					
9	to net cash used by operating activities:					
10	Depreciation					
11	Amortization					
12	Changes in operating assets & liabilites					
13	& liabilities					
14	Accounts Receivable					
15	Inventory					
16	Prepaid Expenses					
17	Other Current Assets					
18	Accounts Payable					
19	Deposits					
20	Line of Credit					
21	Taxes Payable					
22	Other Liabilities					
23						
24	Total Cash used in operating activities	=SUM(B7:B23)	=SUM(C7:C23)	=SUM(D7:D23)	=SUM(E7:E23)	=SUM(F7:F23)
25						
26	Investing Activities:					
27	Net Increase/Decrease in Investment Assets					
28	Net Property & Equipment Activity					
29	Purchase of Intangible Assets					
30						
31	Net Cash used in Investing Activities:	=SUM(B27:B30)	=SUM(C27:C30)	=SUM(D27:D30)	=SUM(E27:E30)	=SUM(F27:F30)
32						
33	Financing Activities					
34	Net Proceeds from Notes Payable					
35	Net Proceeds from Other Long Term Liabilities					
36	Proceeds from the Issuance of Stock					
37	Dividends					
38						
39	Net Cash Used in Financing Activities	=SUM(B34:B38)	=SUM(C34:C38)	=SUM(D34:D38)	=SUM(E34:E38)	=SUM(F34:F38)
40						
41	Net Increase in Cash	=+B24+B31+B39	=+C24+C31+C39	=+D24+D31+D39	=+E24+E31+E39	=+F24+F31+F39
42						
43	*Proof*					
44	Ending Cash	=+'Balance Sheet'!B8	=+'Balance Sheet'!C8	=+'Balance Sheet'!D8	=+'Balance Sheet'!E8	=+'Balance Sheet'!F8
45	Beginning Cash	=+Projection!$B$10	=+'Balance Sheet'!B8	=+'Balance Sheet'!C8	=+'Balance Sheet'!D8	=+'Balance Sheet'!E8
46						
47	Net Increase (Decrease) in Cash	=B44-B45	=C44-C45	=D44-D45	=E44-E45	=F44-F45
48						
49	Difference	=IF(B41-B47=0,"","error")	=IF(C41-C47=0,"","error")	=IF(D41-D47=0,"","error")	=IF(E41-E47=0,"","error")	=IF(F41-F47=0,"","error")

5) Create links to your balance sheet and income statement worksheet
- Operating activities
  - Line 6 operating activities: tie to the income statement: **='Income Statement' !B24**.
  - Changes in operating assets and liabilities usually refer to changes in current assets and liabilities.
  - Accounts receivables, inventory, prepaid expenses and other current assets are all assets (see discussion above). Therefore in column B any balance in year one of the balance sheet are a use of cash and would require a negative balance (i.e., cell B13 would be: **=-'Balance Sheet'!B9** and C13 would be: **='Balance Sheet'!B9-'Balance Sheet'!C9**). This same logic would prevail for all current assets.
  - Accounts payable, deposits, lines of credit, taxes payable and other current liabilities are all liabilities. Therefore in column B any balance in year one of

the balance sheet are a source of cash and would require a positive balance (i.e., cell B17 would be: **='Balance Sheet'!B26** and C17 would be: **='Balance Sheet'!C26-'Balance Sheet'!B26**). Notice again that this is column C minus column B, the exact opposite of an asset. This same logic would prevail for all current liabilities.

- Investing activities
  - On the asset side, investing activities would be those used to buy long-term assets (both tangible and intangible).
  - The logic is just the same as in assets above.
  - If you are buying investments, you would have a negative number (a use of cash); if you are selling investments, you'd have a positive number (a source of cash).
- Financing activities
  - This would be increases in cash from increases in long-term debt and or equity investments. If debt or equity investments are increased, that is a source of cash and therefore a positive number. If you pay back debt or pay dividends (or distributions) that would be indicated by a negative number.
  - As you might deduce, negatives and positives are not necessarily good or bad, they just help numbers people see the story.
  - Again, the formulas are the same as liabilities above.
- Proof
  - The secret to accounting is that everything has to add to zero (Assets-liabilities-equity must equal zero and the sum of all debits minus the sum of all credits must also equal zero.) It is helpful to write formulas to help detect errors in the spreadsheets.
  - Take the ending cash (from the balance sheet and subtract beginning cash from the balance sheet's prior year). That provides the net increase or decrease in cash. Then check to see if that measures the net increase (decrease) in cash as calculated above.
  - Use the formula: **=IF(B40-B46=0,"","error")**. (You should know this formula if you've gotten this far!)

Remember: Neither profit nor cash flow are created by accident. You need a solid idea of where you are going and how you are going to get there. Financial management entails not only the collection and presentation of information, but the *knowledge to interpret and act on that data.*

The Disclaimer

For legal purposes, you want to make absolutely sure whoever is reading your projection knows that these are not guaranteed numbers but an estimate based on the assumptions included on the *Assumptions* page. This one is based on the one used by the American Institute of Certified Public Accountants:

The accompanying financial estimates for YOUR COMPANY NAME reflect managements' judgment, based on present circumstances, of the most likely set of future conditions and the Company's most likely course of action. Selection of the assumptions contained herein required the exercise of managements' judgment.

Deviations from these assumptions, particularly with regard to income, utilization levels, operating expenses, inflation, local taxes, and federal income tax consequences, could significantly affect the projection. Moreover, the actual results are subject to the uncertain effects that changes in economic, legislative, or other circumstances may have on future events.

The financial estimates are provided solely to assist in understanding the potential of YOUR COMPANY NAME, and are not intended to be, and should not be construed as, actual guarantees or predictions of results.

Then sign it (in the name of the company).

Before you show your projections to potential investors, make sure you have a good lawyer to make sure that you are in compliance with applicable state and federal law. Don't skimp on your professional fees. You know the adage: an ounce of prevention is worth a pound of cure. That really holds true in the investment world.

Structuring a Deal

Structuring a deal is as much a science as an art. But before you consider how to structure it, you must determine the following:

- The economics of the deal
- The capital stack
- The weighted cost of capital
- Using the weighted cost of capital in decision-making
- The time value of money
- Structuring the deal

The Economics of the Deal

As we've shown so far, the economics of the deal is concerned with the timing of cash inflows and outflows. This is not an accounting concept, but a time value of money concept. This chapter is dedicated to "making the deal". We are asking the question: "What will make financing the project attractive to a third party?" That third party may be a bank or equity investors or both. The purpose of this chapter is to determine an optimal "capital structure" that rewards all parties in the project.

The Capital Stack

The capital stack is a bird's eye view of the liabilities and equity side of your balance sheet. This is also referred to as the capital structure of your company. Capital structure refers to the way a business entity finances its assets through a combination of equity, debt, or hybrid securities. Suppose we have the capital structure shown in figure 11.1.

Figure 11.1 The capital stack

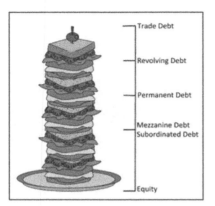

In this example, the liabilities and equity side of the balance sheet includes trade debt (accounts payable), revolving debt (like a line of credit), permanent debt (like a mortgage), mezzanine debt or subordinated debt (like a second mortgage).

The Weighted Cost of Capital

The *weighted cost of capital* (WCC) refers to the cost of a company's funds (both debt and equity). It is a blended rate you pay on all your capital. Suppose that our capital structure is as shown in figure 11.2.

Figure 11.2 Hypothetical capital structure

Accounts Payable	$200,000
Line of Credit	$300,000
Long-term Debt	$2,000,000
Subordinated Debt	$500,000

Total Liabilities	$3,000,000
Stockholders' Equity	$1,000,000

Total Liabilities & Equity	$4,000,000

For an investment to be worthwhile, the expected return on capital (the return on assets) must be greater than the cost of capital.

The cost of debt is simply the rate of interest paid. The cost of equity is more challenging to calculate, as equity does not pay a set return to its investors. It is usually a threshold that would get investors to move their money from one investment to yours.

In figure 11.3, the cost of debt is defined by the instruments securing it. For instance, your accounts payable carry no interest (assuming you pay on time), whereas your long-term debt may be at 6%. The cost of equity is computed based on a variety of risk-related factors (which change over time), but let's assume that your investors expect at 35% return on their money.

Figure 11.3 Capital structure with cost of debt

		Cost
Accounts Payable	$200,000	0%
Line of Credit	$300,000	5%
Long-term Debt	$2,000,000	6%
Subordinated Debt	$500,000	12%

Total Liabilities	$3,000,000	
Stockholders' Equity	$1,000,000	35%

Total Liabilities & Equity	$4,000,000	

The next step is to calculate the percentage of each form of capital with respect to the whole. In other words, accounts payable is $200,000 of the total liabilities and equity of $4,000,000, or 5%. The long-term debt is $2,000,000 of the total liabilities and equity of $4,000,000, or 50% (fig 11.4).

Figure 11.4 The weighted cost of each form of capital

		Cost	Weight
Accounts Payable	$200,000	0%	5%
Line of Credit	$300,000	5%	8%
Long-term Debt	$2,000,000	6%	50%
Subordinated Debt	$500,000	12%	13%

Total Liabilities	$3,000,000		
Stockholders' Equity	$1,000,000	35%	25%

Total Liabilities & Equity	$4,000,000		

Finally, we can calculate the WCC by multiplying the cost by the weight and adding all the weights together. Figure 11.5 shows our weighted cost of capital is 13.63%.

Figure 11.5 The weighted cost of capital

		Cost	Weight	WCC
Accounts Payable	$200,000	0%	5%	0.00%
Line of Credit	$300,000	5%	8%	0.38%
Long-term Debt	$2,000,000	6%	50%	3.00%
Subordinated Debt	$500,000	12%	13%	1.50%

Total Liabilities	$3,000,000			
Stockholders' Equity	$1,000,000	35%	25%	8.75%
	-------------			---------
Total Liabilities & Equity	$4,000,000			13.63%

Using the Weighted Cost of Capital in Decision-Making

The weighted cost of capital is also known as the *hurdle rate*. For our example, when considering whether or not to take on a project, 13.63% is the number the financials need to "clear" in order to be a sound investment.

Once we know the hurdle rate, we can calculate our return on assets (ROA). ROA (or return on investment [ROI]) is the ratio of money gained or lost on an investment relative to the amount of money invested. If the ROA is greater than the cost of capital, you are making money (fig 11.6).

Figure 11.6 When ROA is greater than WCC

Case 1	
Revenue	$5,000,000
EBIT	$700,000
EBIT Margin	14.00%
Total Assets	$4,000,000
ROA	17.50%

In this case, we have revenues of $5,000,000, earnings before interest and taxes (EBIT) of $700,000 for a net profit margin of 14%. We have assets of $4,000,000, so we have a ROA of 17.50%. Since 17.5% is greater than our hurdle rate 13.63%, we are generating equity (our cost of money is less than our return on that money).

In figure 11.7, everything is the same as the last scenario except that our return is $400,000 instead of $700,000. Our net profit margin is 8% ($400,000 divided by $5,000,000) and our ROA is 10% ($400,000 divided by $4,000,000). In this case, our return on capital employed is less than our WCC, and our company is experiencing an erosion of capital.

Figure 11.7 When ROA is less than WCC

Case 2

Revenue	$5,000,000
EBIT	$400,000
EBIT Margin	8.00%
Total Assets	$4,000,000
ROA	10.00%

The Time Value of Money

If a project will last more than one year, there is a concept that takes into consideration the time value of money. This concept means that a dollar today is worth more than a dollar tomorrow.

For example, an investment of $10,000 pays $3,000 for the next five years. Using the IRR function (discounted cash flow) in Excel, we can calculate our internal rate of return (IRR) of 15%. (See page 127 for further discussion.)

Since our hurdle rate is 13.63%, then we would invest in this project. However, if the investment of $10,000 only yields $2,500 per year, then our internal rate of return would be only 8%, meaning that we could not generate enough income to cover our cost of capital.

Structuring the Deal

Once we know what we can afford to pay, now we can consider what we can offer an investor or bank and structure the deal accordingly.

For a straight debt deal, you can pay the bank anything less than your return on investment before interest and taxes. For equity deals, assume you are in a partnership like a limited liability company (LLC), which can be taxed as a partnership. The partnership entity allows you to make unequal distributions and construct any deal you want. There are two allocations in a partnership: profit and cash.

Let's talk about cash allocation. The priority of distributions can be constructed with the following tiers:

■ Priority or preferential return: cash available for distribution will first be distributed so that each member receives a 12% cumulative preferred return on their unreturned capital invested.

■ Return of capital: next, available cash is distributed to the extent of respective unreturned capital.

■ Once cash has been allocated according to the other tiers, then the remaining cash should be distributed in accordance with the profit and loss ratios.

This is just one scenario and you should consult with an attorney and CPA—preferably one with both real estate and partnership taxation expertise. We haven't mentioned the fair market value of assets contributed to a partnership and other more complicated situations. Again, more reason to make sure that you have a good attorney, CPA and a projection to make sure that the math works out.

Other Ways to Get Paid

A projection is absolutely essential when creating an operating agreement. An operating agreement is a formal understanding among members of a company that defines contributions, distributions, profit sharing ratios and a host of other issues involved in running the company. You need to understand the sensitivity of a deal to external factors (slow absorption, change in market conditions, etc.) But, there are other places within the deal for you to make money. Here are a few:

■ Organizational fees: Fees for organizing the legal entity as well as reimbursements for offering expenses.

■ Acquisition stage: Fees based on the purchase price of the property, reimbursement for earnest money, and acquisition expenses.

■ Operating stage: Fees for managing the venture, fees for accounting and tax returns, fees for supervision and/or reimbursements of expenses incurred in connection with the business.

■ Liquidation stage: Fees based on selling price or proceeds from closings, sales fees and/or commissions and, of course, distributions as outlined above.

You've probably heard that no two deals are the same. In my experience, when obtaining money each deal needs to be studied, modeled, and managed. Modeling is so very important to understand the dollars and cents of the transaction and how you turn the investment into a win-win scenario—the investors make money and you make money. If done properly, your investors should be willing to come back and invest with you on future projects.

Creating Your Investor Package

Now that we have discussed the numbers you need to look at when considering a deal and how to structure a deal, let's set up the parameters of an investor package. Open file Ch 11_Structure a Deal found at www.nahb.org/financialforecasting and click on the *Assumptions* page. Although, we have covered the loan situation before, suppose you need money over and above what a lender requires? Our goal now is to create a "deal" that is attractive to an investor.

The first item is to cover the "Participation Requirements." In this case, we'll have the general partner (you), which can also be the organizer, the managing member or anything else you'd like. The second group will be the members, the participants, or the investors.

Figure 11.8 deals with splits. Who is going to put in the initial money? In this scenario, we can say that 90% will be contributed by the investors, and the balance 10% (formula: =1-H14) is 100% (or 1) minus whatever percentage is contributed by the general partner.

Figure 11.8 Priority of distributions chart

Participation Assumptions			
Members:		Investors	GP
Equity Contribution		90.0%	10.0%
Cash Distributions before Preferred & Equity		90.0%	10.0%
Cash Distributions after Preferred & Equity		50.0%	50.0%
Preferred Return on Cash Contributed		14.0%	

As cash comes in, we need to ask two questions:

- If there is positive cash flow, what percentage goes to the investors before they get their initial cash and (if applicable) a preferred return on their cash contributed? In this case (cell H15), they receive 90% of all distributable cash until they get their cash back and a preferred return on their cash of 14%. In advance, the 14% will be calculated based on simple interest, not compounded.

- Then how do you split the additional cash flow after the investors have received their cash investment back and their preferred return money? In this case (cell H16), they receive 50% of all additional distributable cash flow after they've received their cash investment back and their preferred return. The other 50% goes to the general partner.

Almost all investors in a transaction want to be rewarded based on their investment. In this case, we say that their minimum return (if the enterprise can support it) will be 14% (cell H17). Then, once they hit that threshold (their money back and their "guaranteed return"), they will get an additional return (measured as a percentage) of all future cash flow. Ultimately, we can summarize a return as shown in figure 11.9.

Figure 11.9 Summary of investor obligations, return on investment and internal rate of return

	G	H
21	Summary - ROI to Investor	
22	Cash In From GP	80,000
23	Cash In from Investors	720,000
24	Total Cash Out to Investors	901,288
25	Net Cash Generated	181,288
26	Cash on Cash Return	25.20%
27	IRR	19.10%

In our projection, we determined that we needed an investment of $800,000. Of that amount, $720,000 (cell H23) will come from the investors. They'll get back $901,288 (cell H24) which is $181,288 more than they put in (cell H25 with the formula: =H24-H23. The cash on cash return is 25.2% and the formula is: =IFERROR(H24/H23-1,0). The internal rate of return (see page 127) is 19.1%. This formula takes into account the time value of money. Some of these numbers tie to the Equity Analysis. Set this chart up on your *Assumptions* page.

The Equity Analysis

In dealing with an investment, two things can happen: cash comes in (from the investors and general partner) and cash goes out. The equity analysis is divided up into three parts. Part I lists the sources of incoming cash. In our example, we have the investor putting in 90% of the money and the general partner putting in 10%. Part II deals with cash going out; Tier 1 is paying the preferred return first and then returning the principal and Tier 2 is the cash split after the investor gets their preferred return and return of capital. Part III deals with the calculation of IRR.

Cash Contributions

Open the file Chapter 11_ Structure a Deal found at www.nahb.org/financialfore casting and click on the *Equity Analysis* sheet. You will see that the Equity Analysis is already set up, but we have included the detailed instructions here if you want to recreate this on your own.

1) Set up the headers.

- Row 1:
  - Type *Period* in A1.
  - In C1, type the number *1*.
  - In D1, type the formula: **=OFFSET(D1,0,-1)+1**. You could also have typed: **=C1+1**.
  - **Copy** this formula from D1 to N1.
  - Row 2:
- Type *Date* in A2.
  - In B2, type *Totals*.
  - In C2, type in the formula: **=Projection!B6**.
  - **Copy** this formula from C2 to N2.

2) Set up the columns.

We will set up the columns and formulas by the objective of each section. On line 34 of the *Projection* worksheet, we calculated "Funds Needed" and in cells H14 and I14 on the *Assumptions* worksheet we used percentages indicate who was responsible for the "Equity Contributions." In this example we had 90% by the investors and the balance of 10% by the general partner.

- General Partner
  - In cell A3, type *I. Scheduled Cash Contributions*. In cell A4, we want to describe the investor in a manner consistent with the *Assumptions* sheet, cell H13. Type in the formula: **=Assumptions!$H$13**. Thus, if we ever change our title **for our investors**, it will change throughout the projection.
  - In column B, we will have our totals for the project. In cell B4, type in the formula: **=SUM(C4:O4)**. This sums the values in the row.
  - In cell C4, type in the formula: **=Assumptions!$H$14*Projection!B$34**. This takes the investors' percentage equity contribution and multiplies it by funds needed from the *Projection* worksheet. Note that the assumptions reference is an absolute reference. We will always multiply the funds needed by Assumptions!$H$4 (in this case 90%). The reference in projection is to the appropriate column but always line 34.
  - **Copy** that formula across the columns for the projection period.
- Investors
  - In cell A5, we want to describe the owner or general partner (GP) in a manner consistent with the *Assumptions* sheet, cell I13. Type in the formula: **=+Assumptions!$I$13**.

- In column B, we will have our totals for the project. In cell B4, type in the formula: **=SUM(C5:O5)**. This sums the values in the row. We could have just copied cell B4 as these are relative references and would change automatically.

- In cell C4, type in the formula: **=Assumptions!$I$14*Projection!B$34**. This takes the GPs' percentage equity contribution and multiplies it by funds needed from the *Projection* worksheet. Note that the assumptions reference is an absolute reference. We will always multiply the funds needed by Assumptions!$I$14 (in this case 10%).

- **Copy** that formula across the columns for the projection period.

4) Subtotals

- In cell B6, add an apostrophe followed by 7 hyphens ("'-------") and right justify this cell. (Do not put in the quotation marks.) **Copy** it over the appropriate columns.

- Label cell A7 as *Net Cash In*.

- In cell B7, type the formula: **=SUM(B4:B6)**.

Notice the formula in cell B7 includes lines B4:B6, and B6 is the underline. That is on purpose. With the formula like so, if there is a third group of investors, insert a line above line 6. The SUM formula would automatically adjust to **=SUM(B4:B7)**. This eliminates potential errors from incorrect summing formulas. As you work more and more with Excel, you'll learn tricks to minimize your programming and your errors.

When completed, your form will look like the one in figure 11.10 (except that it will be completed through column N):

Figure 11.10 Part 1: Schedule of cash contributions by partner type

	A	B	C	D	E	F
1	Period		1	2	3	4
2	Date	Totals	Jun-14	Jul-14	Aug-14	Sep-14
3	I. Scheduled Cash Contributions					
4	Investors	720,000	720,000	0	0	0
5	GP	80,000	80,000	0	0	0
6		-------	-------	-------	-------	-------
7	Net Cash In	800,000	800,000	0	0	0

Cash Distributions

Now we have set up the cash contributions, we need set up Part II—the distributions. We have two tiers: one before capital and preferred return have been distributed and the other after they've been distributed.

Tier 1 Distributions

1) Enter the row titles as shown in figure 11.11.

Figure 11.11 Calculations of preferred return and return on equity

	A	B
1		Period
2		Date / Totals
9	**II. Cash Available for Distribution**	
10	Cash Available for Distribution	1,100,000
11		
12	**Investors - Preferred Return Calculations**	
13	Preferred Return	70,399
14	Payments	70,399
15		-------
16	Remaining Preferred Return	0
17		
18	**Investors - Return of Capital**	
19	Cash In	720,000
20	Distributions	720,000
21		-------
22	Remaining Principal In	0
23		
24	**Tier 1 Distributions**	
25	Amount to Investors	790,399
26	Amount to GP	87,822
27		-------
28	Total Tier 1 Distributions	878,221
29		-------
30	Amount Remaining to distribute	221,779

- **Copy** the formula from B4 to column B, rows: 10, 13, 14, 19, 20, 25, 26 and row 30.

- Cell A10 is labeled "Cash Available for Distribution," and this is just a link to line 35 on the *Projection* worksheet. The formula in C10 is: **=-Projection!B$35**. Note the relative reference to the column and absolute reference to the row. Also note the minus sign in front of the word Projection! On the *Projection* worksheet, this is a negative number, and on this worksheet it is a positive number. **Copy** the formula through column N.

Now we need to calculate the preferred return. The assumption is that contributions are made in the beginning of the month and the calculation of the distribution is at the end of the month. Because we distribute the preferred return before the cash return, we need to work with the preferred return before the contributions. However, we can't work on the preferred return until we know the contributions. The proverbial chicken and egg dilemma! So, we start at line 13 knowing our formulas won't work until we get to line 28.

2) Payment of Preferred Return

■ The formulas to calculate preferred return and distributions to investors to cover the preferred return are going to reference the *Assumptions* page. Our preferred return is in Assumptions!$H$17. (Note the absolute reference.) The monthly interest is the annual interest (Assumptions!$H$12) divided by 12. The 90% of cash available for distribution (after safety cash) is used to repay the preferred return and return of capital. The 90% is a reference to Assumptions!$H$15. The balance of 10% goes to the general partner (Assumptions!$I$15). The formula in C13 is: **=C19*Assumptions!$H$17/12**. This tells Excel to take the outstanding contribution balance (cash in less distributions that qualify as a return on investment) and multiply it by the monthly interest rate (Assumptions!$H$17/12). **Copy** that formula over to column N.

■ Cell C14 the formula is: **=IF(C$10<=0,0,MIN(Assumptions!$H$15*C$10,C13))**. This says: if there is no cash to distribute then use zero, but if there is, then use the lesser of the distribution percentage before return of capital and preferred return times the cash available (Assumptions!$H$15*C$10) or the amount that is owed (C13).

■ In cell D14, the formula is slightly different: **=IF(D$10<=0,0,MIN(Assumptions! $H$15*D$10,D13+C16))** in that the minimum is the current preferred return (D13) plus the amount still outstanding in the prior period (C16).

■ **Copy** the formula in cell D14 to column N.

■ The formula in C16 (the remaining unpaid preferred return) is simply the amount of preferred return minus any payments: **=C13-C14**. In D16, it is the prior balance plus this month's accrual of preferred return minus the amount paid toward preferred return: **=+C16+D13-D14. Copy** this formula to columns B:N.

In cell B16 (outlined in bold in figure 11.11), the result should be zero if the project generates enough money to pay a preferred return (if it doesn't then you need to change assumptions or abandon the project).

Note: You should see a pattern where the first month of a projection does not carry forward any balances, but the second month through the last month has to take prior balances into consideration.

3) Determine cash in and return of capital for the investors.

■ C19 is a repeat of line 4. In cell C19, the formula is: **=+C4. Copy** this formula to column N.

- The formula in cell C20 is similar to those of C14 the formula is: =IF(C$10<=0,0,MIN(Assumptions!$H$15*C$10-C$14,C19)). This says: If there is no cash to distribute then use zero, but if there is, then use the lesser of the distribution percentage before return of capital and preferred return times the cash available after payment for the preferred return (Assumptions!$H$15*C$10-C$14) or the amount that is owed (C19). There is a little trick going on here. In our example, we take 90% of the cash available minus the money paid in C$14, which is 90% of the amount available. Thus, we are taking only the money available to investors (not all the money) to do our calculation.

- In cell D20, the formula is slightly different: =IF(D$10<=0,0,MIN(Assumptions! $H$15*D$10-D$14,C22+D19)). The minimum is the current outstanding investment (D19) plus the amount still outstanding in the prior period (C22).

- **Copy** the formula in cell D20 to column N.

- The formula in C20 (the remaining unpaid preferred return) is simply the amount of preferred return less any payments: =C13-C14. In D16, it is the prior balance plus this month's capital contributions less the amount paid toward return on capital: =+C16+D13-D14. **Copy** this formula through column N.

In cell B22 (outlined in bold in figure 11.11), the result should be zero if the project generates enough money to return an investor's capital (if it doesn't then you need to change assumptions or abandon the project).

4) Determine the balance of unreturned capital.

- In cell C22, the formula is: =+C19-C20. This is a little different. **Copy** this formula from *B22* to N22.

5) Aggregate amount paid to investors and determine the amount paid to the general partner

- In cell A25, type in the formula: ="**Amount to** "&$A$4. Text goes between quotation marks and is connected to variables by the "&". Note there is a space between "to" and the closing quotation mark.

- In cell A26, type in the formula: ="**Amount to** "&$A$5.

- Line 25 will add the totals paid to the investor on lines 14 and 20 for preferred return and return of capital respectively. The formula is: =+C14+C20. **Copy** that through column N.

- If you recall, we worked with the "Cash distributions before preferred" in order to make sure we were at 90%. So, whatever was paid to the investor represented 90% of the money available for distribution. Now, calculate the amount available to the general partner with the following formula: =(C25/ Assumptions!$H$15)*Assumptions!$I$15. This says: take the amount paid to the investors and divide it by their distribution percentage (C25/Assumptions!$H$15). The result is 100% of the money allocated for Tier 1 distributions. Then multiply this by the amount that goes to the general partner (Assumptions!$I$15). As in algebra, the use of parenthesis is absolutely critical to these formulas as this tells the computer the order of calculations.

■ Line 28 is the total of all distributions paid to the investors and the general partner. The formula is: **=SUM(C25:C27)**. **Copy** that formula from column B:N.

6) Determine the amount available for Tier 2 distributions.

■ The formula is: **=+C10-C28**. This says take all the cash available for distribution minus the amount paid for Tier 1 distributions.

Tier 2 Distributions

Tier 1 distributions are the hardest to calculate. There are many alternatives like compounded interest, different break points, etc. The permutations are limited only by your imagination. Tier 2 distributions simply ask the question, "Once I get back my money and preferred distributions, what's in it for me?" This may be referred to by some as the "equity kicker."

In our case, the equity kicker is defined on the *Assumptions* page. Cell G16 refers to cash distributions after equity and preferred returns: 50% goes to the investors (Assumptions!$H$16) and 50% (what's left) to the general partner (Assumptions!$I$16).

1) On the *Equity Analysis* page, set up the row labels.

■ Cell A33 is "Amount to Investors." The formula is: **="Amount to "&$A$5.** (The same as line 25.)

■ Cell A34 is "Amount to GP." The formula is: **="Amount to "&$A$5.** (The same as line 26.)

The *Assumptions* page has the amount paid to participants after the return of equity and the preferred return. The amount to investors is Assumptions!$H$16 and the amount to the general partner is Assumptions!$I$16

2) Distribute the remaining money to investors

■ The formula in A33 is: **="Amount to "&$A$4**

■ The formula in B33 is: **=SUM(C33:O33)**. This is the sum of the amounts disbursed to investors.

■ The formula in C33 is: **=Assumptions!$H$16*C30**. This says take the amount to be distributed to investors and multiply it by the distributable cash.

■ **Copy** this formula over to column N.

3) Distribute the remaining money to the general partner

- The formula in A34 is: ="Amount to "&$A$5
- The formula in B34 is: =SUM(C34:O34). This is the sum of the amounts disbursed to GP.
- The formula in C34 is: =C30-C33. This says take the amount to be distributed minus the amount paid to investors and distribute that to the general partner.
- **Copy** this formula over to column N.

Internal Rate of Return

When looking at an investment, investors consider the time value of money, which compares a cash outflow at the beginning of a proposed project with the anticipated cash inflows to be generated by the project. A valid comparison cannot be made using absolute dollar amounts because money has a time value. (i.e., $100 today is worth more than $100 two years from now.)

Many investors use the internal rate of return (IRR) to analyze an investment. This calculation returns the rate of interest that makes the net present value of an income stream equal to zero. That is, the IRR of an investment is the discount rate at which the net present value of costs (negative cash flows) equals the net present value of the benefits (positive cash flows).

The bottom line is that the greater the IRR, the better the project in question (for the investor). A firm (or individual) should, in theory, undertake all projects or investments available with IRRs that exceed the cost of capital (the hurdle rate).

IRR and XIRR functions

That being said, this calculation is done in Excel for us. IRR function returns the internal rate of return for a series of cash flows represented by the numbers. These cash flows can vary in amount but must happen at regular intervals. The internal rate of return is the interest rate received for an investment consisting of payments (negative values) and income (positive values) that occurs at regular periods. The syntax of IRR is as follows: **=IRR(values, [guess])**

The values are represented by an array. This group of cells must contain at least one positive and one negative value. If an array or reference argument contains text, logical values, or empty cells, those values are ignored. The guess is just that: it is your guess as to what the IRR may be. This is optional, but it is fun to put in anyway.

Again, the biggest assumption is that the flows are at regular intervals. If you want to know the internal rate of return for cash flows that are not periodic, then use XIRR. This is very much like IRR except in the syntax: **=XIRR(values, dates, guess)**

This is the same as IRR except that the dates are a schedule of payment dates that correspond to the cash flow payments. The dates need to be entered through the DATE function (i.e., DATE(2014,6,1) for June 1, 2014).

The Equity Analysis – ROI

We are ready for the last section of the *Equity Analysis* sheet. This is critical in understanding how to present this to an investor. If you don't have an attractive return on investment, then you need to ask yourself whether or not this venture should be initiated. On the other hand, if the return is too high, then restructure it to make it more attractive to yourself.

SUMIFS Function

We covered SUMIF in Chapter 9 Equity Needs, page 75. Now, let's introduce you to SUMIFS. SUMIFS adds the cells in a range that meet multiple criteria. For example, if you want to sum the numbers in the range C44:N44 only if the corresponding numbers in C51:N51 are equal to 2014 (the year) and the corresponding numbers in C44:N44 are greater than 0, you can use the following formula: **=SUMIFS(C40:N40, C51:N51, "2014", C40:N40, ">0")**. Note that the formula has matching column headings (C and N). This doesn't always have to be true, but this function can be tricky. The syntax is:

=SUMIFS(sum_range, criteria_range1, criteria1, [criteria_range2, criteria2], ...)

Sum_range is one or more cells to sum. Cell references that contain blanks and text values are ignored. Criteria_range1 is the first range in which to evaluate the associated criteria, and the criteria is the criteria in the form of a number, expression, cell reference, or text that define which cells in the *criteria_range1* argument will be added. For example, criteria can be expressed as 32, ">32", B4, "apples," or "32." Criteria_range2, criteria2 are optional. Up to 127 range/criteria pairs are allowed.

1) Enter the row labels.

- In cell A39, enter the label *III. Equity Analysis – ROI*
- In cell A40, enter the formula: **="Cash flow to the "&+Assumptions!$H$13**. Note that the text portion is in quotation marks.
- In cell A42, enter *Internal Rate of Return.*
- In cell A48, enter the formula: **="Cash flow to the "&+Assumptions!$I$13**. Note that the text portion is in quotation marks.
- In cell A49, enter *Cash Flow by Year.*
- In cell A50, enter *Internal Rate of Return.*
- On line 52, we are going to test that everything is in balance. If it's in balance, we will see zero (everything going into and out of the enterprise is equal). In cell A48, we enter the difference.
- In cell A49, enter *Cash Proof.*
- In cell A55, enter in *Year.* (You'll see the benefit of this in below.)

2) Analyze the IRR to the investors.

- On line 40, we will analyze the cash flow to the investor. Cell B40 contains the formula: **=SUM(C40:O40)** and C40 contains the formula: **=-C4+C25+C33**. This subtracts the money coming into the investment from investors (negative values) and adds any distributions from Tier 1 and Tier 2. This formula is copied through the column N.

- In cell C55, (this is the Year we talked about in step 1), type the formula: **=YEAR(C2)**. This gives us the year, and we format it to be a number with zero decimals and uncheck the "Use 1000 Separator(,)" box. This year will create one of the criteria we need to do internal rate of return. (As we mentioned, the IRR calculation deals with regular-time intervals. This is important to remember as this may impact the return we recognize.)

- In cell B41, enter the formula: **=SUMIF($C40:$N40,"<=0")**. This formula says the take the sum of all receipts (remember receipts from the investor are negative numbers) to determine the net investment into the project. This formula needs to be challenged as the timeframes move from 1 year to multiple years.

- In C41, we want to calculate all the cash distributed to the investor during the first year of the projections. The formula is:

  **=SUMIFS($C$40:$N$40,$C$51:$N$51,YEAR(Assumptions!$B$5),
  $C$40:$N$40,">0").**

  This says: add the numbers in the range C40:N40 only if the corresponding numbers in C51:N51 are equal to 2014 (the year) and the corresponding numbers in C40:N40 are greater than 0. But, unlike the formula in the discussion of IRR, instead of putting in the year 2014, we put in YEAR(Assumptions!$B$5) which gives us the year 2014 in this example but again, everything is dynamic instead of fixed.

- In D41, enter the formula:

  **=SUMIFS($C$40:$N$40,$C$51:$N$51,YEAR(Assumptions!$B$5)
  +1,$C$40:$N$40,">0").**

  This is the same as formula in C41 except that we use YEAR(Assumptions! $B$5)+1 so the year adjusts to 2015. We can copy this formula over incrementing +1 to +2 to +3 until we have enough to cover each year of our projection.

- In cell B42, calculate the IRR with the following formula: **=IFERROR(IRR (B41:E41,0),0)**. We put the IRR formula within the IFERROR command so if there is an error, the cell will show a zero.

3) A detour to XIRR for purposes of showing you the difference between XIRR and IRR

- In cell A44, type in *Dates.*
- In cell A45, type in *Cash Flow by Year.*
- In cell A46, type in *Internal Rate of Return (uneven periods).*
- In cell B44, type in the formula: **=Assumptions!B5**. That is the starting date.
- In cell C44, type in the formula: **=DATE(YEAR(B44),12,31)**, which is December 31 of the year of the project's inception.
- In cell C45, type in the formula: **=DATE(YEAR(C44)+1,12,31)**, which is the year end of the next year. **Copy** this formula over to capture every year of your projection.
- In cell B45, type in the formula: **=B41** for the money into the project, and **copy** this formula over for each of the applicable years
- Finally in cell B46, type in the formula: **=XIRR(B45:E45,B44:E44,0.1)**. Now this formula yields a return of 19.1%, which is higher than the 14.1% in cell B42 because we took into effect the actual dates. This is a very different story to your investors than just IRR. However, the effects diminish the longer the project is.

4) Analyze the IRR to the general partners.

- On line 48, we will calculate the cash flow to the general partner. Cell B48 contains the formula: **=SUM(C48:O48)** and C48 contains the formula: **=-C5+C26+C34**, which subtracts the money coming into the investment from the general partners (negative values) and adds any distributions from Tier 1 and Tier 2. This formula is copied through the column N.
- In cell B49, enter the formula: **=SUMIF($C48:$N48,"<=0")**. This formula says: take the sum of all receipts to determine the net investment into the project. This formula needs to be changed in cells C49 and further out as the timeframes move from 1 year to multiple years.
- In C49, we want to calculate all the cash distributed to the investor during the first year of the projections. The formula is:

$$=\text{SUMIFS(\$C\$48:\$N\$48,\$C\$55:\$N\$55,YEAR}$$
$$\text{(Assumptions!\$B\$5),\$C\$48:\$N\$48,">0")}.$$

This says: add the numbers in the range C48:N48 only if the corresponding numbers in C55:N55 are equal to 2014 (the year) and the corresponding numbers in C48:N48 are greater than 0. But unlike the formula in the discussion of IRR, instead of putting in the year 2014, we enter YEAR(Assumptions!$B$5).

This gives us the year 2014 in this example but again, everything is dynamic instead of fixed.

■ In D49, we have the formula:

$$=SUMIFS(\$C\$48:\$N\$48,\$C\$55:\$N\$55,YEAR$$
$$(Assumptions!\$B\$5)+1,\$C\$48:\$N\$48,">0").$$

This is the same as in cell C49 except that we use YEAR(Assumptions!$B$5)+1 so the year adjusts to 2015. We can copy this formula over incrementing +1 to +2 to +3 until we have enough to cover each year of our projection.

■ In cell B50, calculate the IRR with the following formula: **=IFERROR(IRR (B49:E49,0),0)**. We put the IRR formula within the IFERROR command so if there is an error, the cell will show a zero. You can get an error if the GP doesn't contribute cash to the project.

5) Make sure all the cash coming into and out of the project are accounted for.

This step is probably the most critical. In most projections, people look to see if numbers match. Train yourself to look for zeros, program to make sure everything is accounted for.

■ In cell B52, enter the formula: **=SUM(C52:N52)**. This sum should be zero, and this means that the monthly cash is all accounted for.

■ In cell C52, enter the formula: **=C36-C48-C40**. This calculates the net cash flow of the enterprise (or project) minus the cash flow to investors and the general partners. This should equal zero. **Copy** this across to column N.

■ In accounting there is a concept of footing and cross-footing. That means that the sum of the rows (row totals – column B) should equal the sum of the columns (line 48). The formula is: **=+B36-B40-B48**. That is, the net cash flow (or profit) minus the next cash flow to the investors and general partners must equal zero.

How do you raise money?

For nearly as long as humans have used money, we have borrowed other people's money. And through banks' centuries of experience of holding one person's money and lending it to another, they've gotten very good at deciding when it makes sense to lend. They know what they're looking for. Your job as a business owner is to position yourself as the kind of business they want to see.

You do this by assembling a loan or investor package. While a loan package is made up of a number of complex financial documents, it essentially addresses four basic questions:

- How much money do you require?
- When do you need the money?
- How will you repay the money?
- What is the risk?

While most of us might think that the fourth question is the most important, think about the third. Ask yourself this before you move on to the next chapter: how will you pay your investors back? More importantly, how will you *demonstrate* that you can pay them back?

Sensitivity Analysis 12

I have yet to meet a banker or investor who doesn't ask, "What if?" They always look for worst-case scenarios. We counter that by determining what the right deal is for an investor, and then using our projection to justify that outcome.

An elevator speech refers to the idea that you can tell a stranger what you do during the course of an elevator ride. If they are interested, you can continue. If not, you go on to your next prospect. The same is true of an investment. You don't want to bombard an investor with all the calculations that we've done throughout the book. Start with the equivalent of an elevator speech. If they are interested, they will ask you for more information. If not, move on to the next investor.

The Back-of-the-Napkin Analysis

You should be able to summarize the financial feasibility of a project on the back of a napkin. Open Chapter 12_Sensitivity Analysis at www.nahb.org/financialfore casting and click on the *Assumptions* sheet. You will see the Summary – Project box as shown in figure 12.1.

Figure 12.1 Back-of-the-napkin project summary

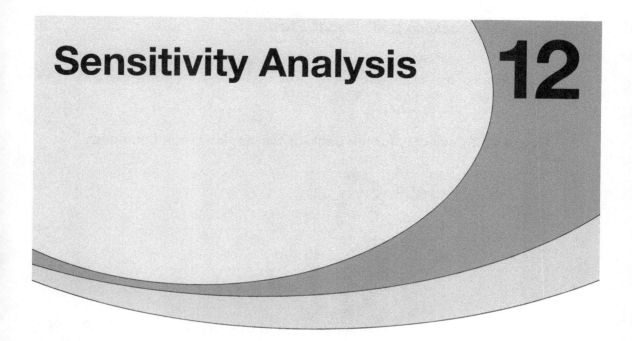

	G	H
29	**Summary - Project**	
30	Gross Revenues	3,600,000
31	Cost of Goods Sold	2,850,000
32	Gross Profit	750,000
33	Financing Costs	162,000
34	Marketing Costs	144,000
35	General & Administrative Costs	144,000
36	Net Profit	300,000

It summarizes the gross revenues, costs, and net profits. Fairly easy so far! The formulas are shown in figure 12.2.

Figure 12.2 Formulas for the back-of-the-napkin project summary

	G	H
29	**Summary - Project**	
30	Gross Revenues	=+Projection!N14
31	Cost of Goods Sold	=SUM(Projection!N21:N23
32	Gross Profit	=+H30-H31
33	Financing Costs	=+Projection!N24
34	Marketing Costs	=+Projection!N25
35	General & Administrative Costs	=+Projection!N26
36	Net Profit	=+H32-SUM(H33:H35)

For the most part, the formulas are links to selective totals on the *Projection* sheet. Next, we want to summarize the projection from the investor's point of view (fig 12.3).

Figure 12.3 Summary of investor obligations, return on investment and internal rate of return

	G	H
21	**Summary - ROI to Investor**	
22	Cash In From GP	80,000
23	Cash In From Investors	720,000
24	Total Cash Out to Investors	901,288
25	Net Cash Generated	181,288
26	Cash on Cash Return	25.2%
27	IRR	19.1%

The summary formulas are shown in figure 12.4.

Figure 12.4 Formulas for figure 12.3

	G	H
21	**Summary - ROI to Investor**	
22	="Cash In From "&$I$13	=-'Equity Analysis'!$B$49
23	="Cash In From "&$H$13	=-'Equity Analysis'!B41
24	Total Cash Out to Investors	=SUM('Equity Analysis'!C41:E41)
25	Net Cash Generated	=+H24-H23
26	Cash on Cash Return	=IFERROR(H24/H23-1,0)
27	IRR	='Equity Analysis'!B46

Again, fairly easy! Just linking!

Data Tables

What if you think an IRR of 19.1% is too much, or too little? Then you should create a data table that shows you the returns based on varying certain assumption.

Let's create a simple analysis. Open a new workbook and fill in the fields A1:D1 and A2:C2 as shown in figure 12.5. We can calculate the PMT on a loan by entering the principal, the interest, and the term. Always note the applicable units; the interest rate is per annum, but the term is in months. The PMT command must match apples with apples. The formula in D2 is: **=PMT(B2/12,C2,A2)**. We divide the interest rate by 12 to make it monthly. Our result is a monthly payment of $84.99. But what if we borrowed $5,000 or $6,000, or what if we paid 11%, 12% or 13%? Figure 12.5 illustrates how Excel allows us to create a table showing the alternatives in one table.

Figure 12.5 An example of a data table

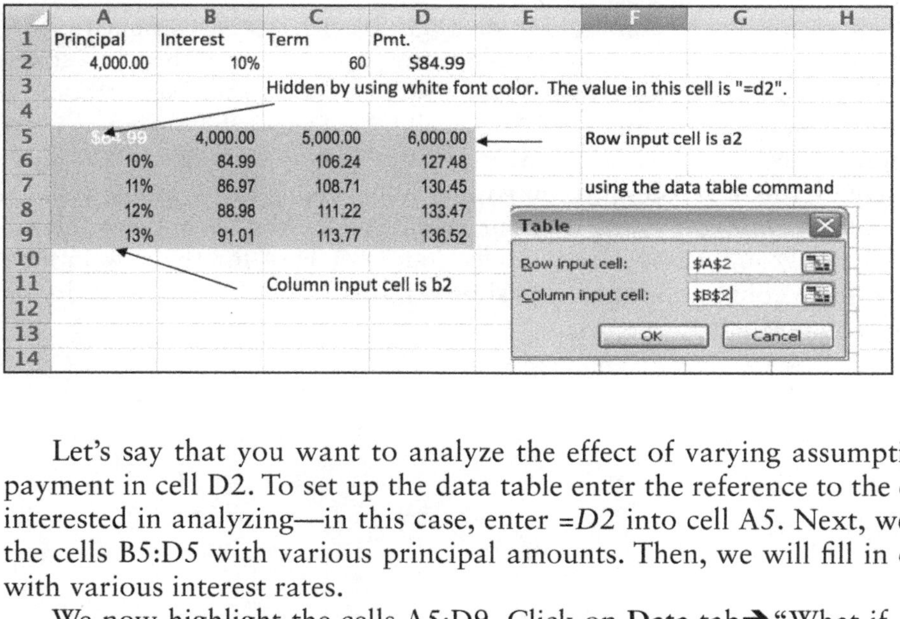

Let's say that you want to analyze the effect of varying assumptions on the payment in cell D2. To set up the data table enter the reference to the cell you are interested in analyzing—in this case, enter *=D2* into cell A5. Next, we will fill in the cells B5:D5 with various principal amounts. Then, we will fill in cells A6:A9 with various interest rates.

We now highlight the cells A5:D9. Click on **Data** tab➔"What if analysis"➔ Data Table. The row input is the cell in which the principal amounts will be entered ($A$2), and the column inputs are where the interest rate would be entered ($B$2). Hit OK, and the table is filled out for you. You'll see formulas within the table that look like this: {**=TABLE(A2,B2)**} where the brackets tell Excel it is using an array formula.

Sensitivity Analysis on the Investment

Now back to the *Assumptions* page in the Chapter 12_Sensitivity Analysis workbook. We now can do a sensitivity analysis on our internal rate of return given different equity contributions (cell H14) and different preferred returns (cell H17). The results are shown in figure 12.6

Figure 12.6 Sensitivity analysis for the IRR

	L	M	N	O
21	**Sensitivity on Equity**			
22	19.1%	90.0%	80.0%	70.0%
23	10.0%	18.2%	12.5%	5.2%
24	12.0%	18.7%	12.9%	5.2%
25	14.0%	19.1%	13.3%	5.2%
26	16.0%	19.6%	13.7%	5.2%

Cell M25 is outlined in bold to highlight the 19.1% based on a 14% preferred return and a 90% distribution before the investor recovered their investment back.

The Sensitivity on Equity box already appears on the *Assumptions* sheet. To create it from scratch, enter =H27 into cell L22. That is the result we are trying to optimize. Next, put various equity contributions on cells M22:O22 and various preferred returns in column L on rows 23:26. Highlight the range L22:O26, and click on the **Data** tab in the tool bar, then click on the "What If Analysis" in the Data Tools group. Choose data table, and enter H14 for the row input cell and H17 for the column input cell, as shown in figure 12.7. Hit **OK** and viola! Your table is complete.

Figure 12.7 Setting up the table parameters

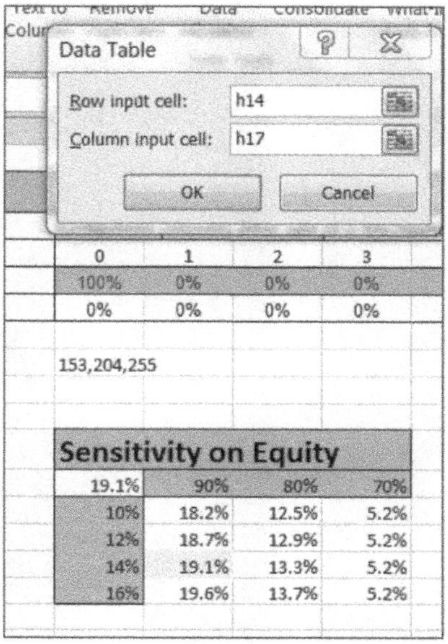

Now, armed with this table, you can determine what you want to offer the investor, and as they counter your offer, you can quickly assess what you are willing to give up.

The Complete Construction Projection

13

Now we are ready to assemble this projection and make it presentation ready. In this chapter, we will talk about creating the capital request, creating a graph for easy presentation of our data and tricks to print out worksheets in presentation view.

Assembling and Presenting the Capital Request

Once you have decided on a funding approach and done the necessary gathering and research, as outlined in this book, you can begin the assembly and presentation process.

A financing package should either be professionally bound or neatly assembled in a quality three-ring notebook and labeled with your business name. Also, you could send it electronically in a PDF (however, don't skimp on the organization of your documents within the PDF). If you are sending it electronically, please make sure you have human interaction because a lot of debt and/or equity decision is based on a personal relationship. In general, structure the package in the following order:

- Simple cover page with a title, the date, and your contact information
- A terms sheet (see below) that sums up who you are, what you are asking for, what you will do with what you receive, and how you intend to repay the loan
- Table of contents
- Body
- Sectional tabs (Though not absolutely necessary, it helps readers to find information.)

Beyond that, it's not just what you say, but how you say it. The more professional you come across, the more the bank and/or investor will be impressed. Presentation matters! When presenting a package to a banker or investor, there is only one opportunity to make a good impression.

Believe it or not, investors like to see pictures, particularly in the building and real estate industries. They're human, after all, and they respond to visuals as much as they respond to content. Include pictures, renderings, models, and anything else. If necessary, hire a designer to make your request look professional.

One of the best ways of illustrating financial data is to chart it. Excel makes charting easy. Charts are linked directly to your data so that changes appear instantly.

Let's say that we want to chart Gross Sales, Cost of Goods Sold, and Operating Expenses. Open the Chapter13_The Complete Construction Projection workbook at www.nahb.org/financialforecasting and click on the *Chart* sheet. As with previous chapters, the file on the website has all the formulas and information included, but we are giving you step-by-step instructions so that you can understand and apply the formulas from scratch.

1) Set up the columns.

- Open a new workbook page and title the tab *Chart*.
- Link cell B1 to cell B6 on the *Projection* page.
- **Copy** that formula across the applicable columns.

2) Set up the rows.

- Label cell A2 *Gross Sales,* cell A3 *Cost of Goods Sold,* and cell A4 *Operating Expenses.*

3) Set up the values.

- In cell B2, enter the formula: **=Projections!B43**.
- In cell B3, enter the formula: **=-Projection!B49** (the minus is to make it a positive number).
- In cell B4, enter the formula: **=SUM(Projection!B24:B26)**
- **Copy** cells B2:B4 across the appropriate columns.

4) Determine what data you want to chart and create a table.

5) Pick a chart.

- Highlight the data you want to include on the chart.
- Go to the **Insert** tab (fig 13.1) and select a chart.

Figure 13.1 Selecting a chart type

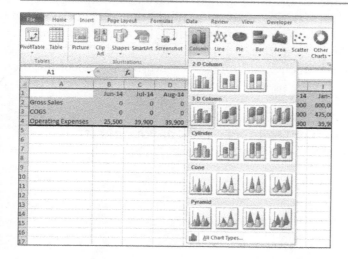

TIP: Highlight the data (A1:M4) on the *Chart* sheet and then click on a chart type. In figure 13.1 we selected a column chart and it displayed related charts. Hit **Enter** and you should have a screen like the one shown in figure 13.2.

Figure 13.2 The chart automatically created by Excel

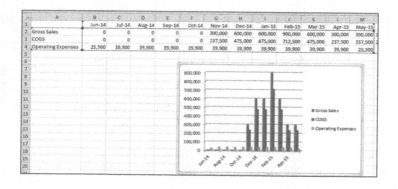

6) Customize your chart.

■ Highlight the chart and a pop-menu called "Chart Tools" appears with 3 tabs: **Design, Layout** and **Format.** On the **Format** tab in the Current Selection group (on the far left side), click the arrow next to the Chart Area box, and then click the chart element that you want to work with (in figure 13.3, the Chart Area is selected). Once selected, click on Format Selection, then select fill, then solid fill and pick a color.

Figure 13.3 Working with different elements of your chart

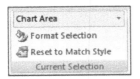

■ On the **Layout** tab, you can do the one or more of the following:
   • In the Labels group (fig 13.4), click the Label layout option that you want.

Figure 13.4 Working with the Labels group on the Layout tab

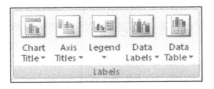

   • For instance, click on Chart Title➔select above chart, type in your title and then resize.
   • If you want to create a vertical or horizontal axis title, click on Axis Titles.
      ◊ Click on Axis Title➔Primary Horizontal Title➔and choose one of the options.
      ◊ Click on Axis Title➔Primary Vertical Title➔and choose one of the options.

■ In the Axes group (fig 13.5), click the axis or gridline option that you want.

Figure 13.5 Working with the Axes group on the Layout tab

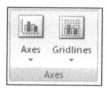

- Primary Horizontal Axis➔show left to right axis
- Primary Vertical Axis➔show default axis
- Click more options, which allows you to customize the scale.

■ In the Background group (fig 13.6), click the layout option that you want.

Figure 13.6 Working with the Background group on the Layout tab

7) Customize your headings.

■ On the Chart Layout tab, click chart title, then in the input area on the top of the page, type a cell reference, (i.e., **=Assumptions!$A$1**), which contains the company name.

■ To include multiple lines on a title, select a random, unused cell. In this case, enter the following formula in cell N7: **=Assumptions!A1&CHAR(10)& "Sales"**. The CHAR(10) reference is for a carriage return.

■ Select the chart title (the outline of the text box *not* the contents of the text box itself).

■ On a chart, click the chart or axis title that you want to link to a worksheet cell.

■ On the worksheet, click in the formula bar and type an equal sign (=).

■ Select the worksheet cell that contains the data or text that you want to display in your chart.

TIP: You can also type the reference to the worksheet cell in the formula bar. Include an equal sign, the sheet name (this is required even if the cell is on the same worksheet as the chart as they are both separate "objects"), followed by an exclamation point; for example, =Sheet1!F2 or in our case =Chart!$N$7. Press **Enter.**

If you want to make any changes to the chart, **right click** on the chart and get a menu as shown in figure 13.7.

Figure 13.7 Making changes to your chart

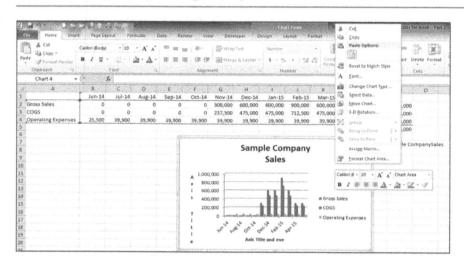

This is just one of many charts. I encourage you to try various charts, especially bar and pie charts.

Previewing and Printing Your Data

As you prepare your financial package for potential investors, you will need print copies of the worksheets you created in Excel. Printing from Excel can be as easy as hitting the **Print** button, or it can be quite complicated if you want to print only selected regions of your worksheet.

Print the Entire Worksheet

To print all of a worksheet, click in the worksheet. On the Quick Access Toolbar, click the **Print** button as circled in figure 13.8.

Figure 13.8 To print a worksheet click on the Print button on Quick Access Toolbar.

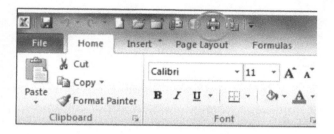

There are several ways to print a document, as shown in figure 13.9:

- On the **File** tab, click Print.
- Under Settings, click Print Selection.
- Click the **Print** button.

Figure 13.9 If you want more control over what is being printed go to the File tab, select Print Option and set up your print parameters before hitting the Print button.

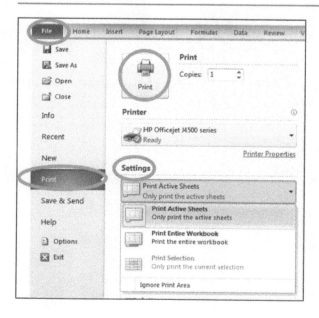

Controlling Printed Output

You can use the **Page Layout** tab to make changes to your printout without changing your sheet. For example, you can specify:

- Page orientation (landscape or portrait)
- Headers and footers
- Printing a range or multiple ranges
- Hiding rows and columns
- Printing titles

Orientation

Figure 13.10 shows how you can set the page orientation to portrait (tall pages) or landscape (wide pages). Use landscape when you have a lot of columns (especially when you have 12 months to show on one page).

Figure 13.10 Using the Page Layout tab to determine orientation of the print out

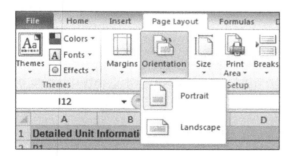

Or you can go to the **Print Titles** icon in the Page Setup Group and open up the dialog box (fig 13.11) and click on the **Page** tab.

Figure 13.11 An alternative method of choosing a page orientation

Headers and Footers

Headers and footers are lines of text that print at the top or bottom of each page, respectively. They are not seen in "normal" view but are visible in "page layout" view. They are used to add information to a spreadsheet that is being printed, such as titles, dates, and/or page numbers.

A header or footer can contain up to three pieces of information, which can appear in three locations:

■ Header information can be placed on the top-left corner, the top-center, and the top-right corner of the page.

■ Footer information can be placed on the bottom-left corner, the bottom-center, and the bottom-right corner of the page.

There are two ways to access headers and footers:

1.) On the Insert tab:

In the Text group (fig 13.12), click Header & Footer.

Figure 13.12 Creating headers and footers on the Insert tab

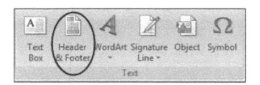

When you click on this button, the screen will go into print layout mode. The "Header & Footer Elements" tab will pop up. You can enter your own text and/or use predefined elements for your headers and footers. The predefined elements on the ribbon are shown in figure 13.13:

Figure 13.13 Menu of predefined header and footer elements

Clicking on predefined elements will insert

- Page Number: The page number
- Number of Pages: Inserts the total number of pages
- Current Date or Current Time: The print date or time of day
- File Path: The "address" of the file on your computer
- File Name, or Sheet Name: The file information.
- Picture: A graphic image.
- Format Picture: Resize, rotate, or crop a header or footer graphic image.

To exit print layout mode, click a cell within the active worksheet, click the **View** tab and then click "Normal" in the Workbook Views group. In normal view, you may see page breaks as black dotted lines. In order to hide page breaks, go to File, select Options at the bottom right side of the menu bar, select advanced in the left column scroll down to Display, then find a category called "Display options for this worksheet" and unclick "Show page breaks". Because this is so cumbersome, I prefer the next option.

2.) On the **Page Layout** tab:

■ Click Print Titles in the Page Setup group, which brings up the Page Setup pop-up menu, and click on the Header/Footer tab (fig 13.14).

Figure 13.14 Creating headers and footers on the Page Layout tab in the Page Setup group

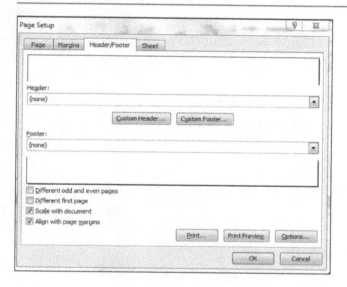

■ Click the **Custom Header** or **Custom Footer** button (fig 13.15), and click the buttons to insert the information that you want in that section. A header or footer can have up to three sections: left, right and center.

Figure 13.15 The header popup allows you to work with the three sections.

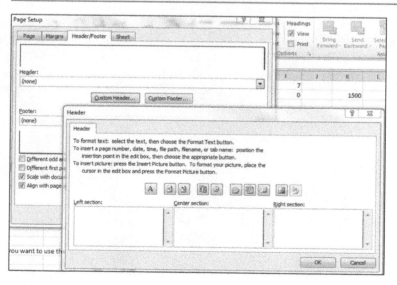

■ If you don't want to use the predefined elements in your footer, you can change the header or footer text by editing the existing text in the Left section, Center section, or Right section box.

Print a Range of Data

This is a little different than printing a whole page:

■ Click the **Page Layout** tab.

■ Return to the worksheet, and then select the range of data that you want to print.

■ Method 1:
  • Click Print Area and then Set Print Area from the drop-down menu.
  • Click the **Print** Button on the Quick Access Toolbar.

■ Method 2:
  • On the **File** tab, click Print.
  • Under Settings, click Print Selection.
  • Click Print.

Hiding Rows or Columns

There are two ways to hide or unhide rows:

■ Select the rows you want to hide by clicking on the column letter(s) or row number(s). Then **right click**, which brings up the pop up menu (fig 13.16) and select Hide.

Figure 13.16 Hiding rows or columns

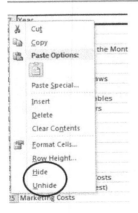

■ On the **Home** tab, in the Cells group, click Format. Then, in the Visibility group point to Hide & Unhide. Unhide is a toggle if you select the rows above and below the row that is hidden or to the right and left of the columns that are hidden (fig 13.17).

Figure 13.17 Rows 5 and 7 are hidden.

	A	B	C	D	E
1			Sample Company		
2			Cash Flow Statement		
3					
4	Period	1	2	3	4
6	Month	Jun-14	Jul-14	Aug-14	Sep-14
8	Sales in Units				

Repeat Specific Rows or Columns on Every Printed Page

If a worksheet spans more than one page, you can print row and column headings or labels (also called print titles) on every page to help make sure that the data is correctly labeled.

■ Select the worksheet that you want to print.

■ On the **Page Layout** tab, in the Page Setup group, click Print Titles (fig 13.18). This brings up the Page Setup dialog box (fig 13.19).

Figure 13.18 The Print Titles button in the Page Setup group on the Page Layout tab

Figure 13.19 Page Setup dialog box

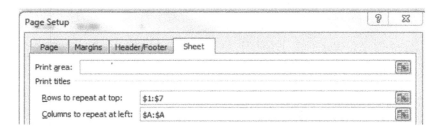

Click on the Sheet tab of the dialog box. You will use the area called Print Titles. To repeat rows on the top, enter the reference of the rows that contain the column labels. To repeat columns on the left, enter the reference of the columns that contain the row labels that you want. For example, if you want to print column labels at the top of every printed page, enter: **$1:$7** in the rows to repeat at top box.

Printing Multiple Ranges on a Sheet

Let's say you have a projection that covers 24 months. You might want to print one year at a time and have the same titles and columns on both sheets. In this case, you would determine the multiple ranges you want and insert those ranges in the print area. Separate each print area by a comma. So, let's suppose our data is in cells B8:Y37 and year 1.

To set the print area on your worksheet using the Print Area menu item, follow these steps:

- Select the range of cells that you want to set as your print area.
- On the File menu, point to Print Area, and then click Set Print Area.

Note: You can clear an existing print area by repeating the first two steps, and then clicking Clear Print Area.

For the second area, do the same:

- Select the next range of cells that you want to set as your print area.
- On the **Page Layout** tab, click Print Area, and then click Add to Print Area.

The Print Titles dialog box is shown in figure 13.20.

Figure 13.20 Printing multiple ranges from one worksheet

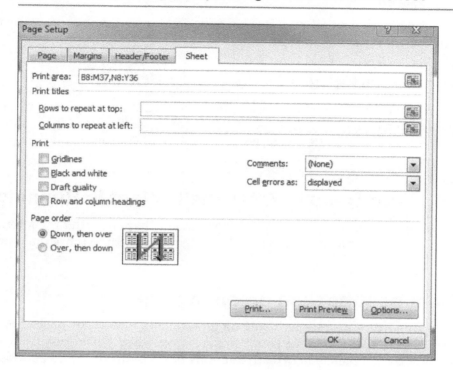

Or you could have just typed in B37:M37, N8:Y36. But what would happen if you type B37:M37, N8:Y37? Since all cells are contiguous (next to each other and perfectly aligned), Excel would override the Print Area to B8:Y37.

Fixing Awkward Page Breaks

Your worksheet data may be too wide or too long to fit on one page, or perhaps you want to keep specific data together on the same page. You can use View➔Page Break Preview to quickly adjust the vertical and horizontal page breaks. In this view, page breaks that are manually inserted appear as solid lines. Dashed lines indicate where page breaks are displayed automatically. To move a page break, drag the page break to a new location. Moving the automatic page bread changes it to a manual page break.

■ On the **View** tab, click Page Break Preview.

■ Then you can do any of the following:

• To insert a vertical or horizontal page break, select a row or column below or to the right of where you want to insert the page break, **right click**, and then click Insert Page Break.

- To remove a page break, **drag** the page break outside of the page break preview area.
- To remove all manual page breaks, **right click** any cell on the worksheet, and then click Reset All Page Breaks.

Previewing a Worksheet Before You Print It

Use Print Preview to view your work before printing, make adjustments, and see the results immediately. Go to the **View** tab, and in the Workbook Views Group and click Page Layout. In this view, you can view both your work and the preview at the same time.

Comparing Your Results After the Project is Running

The final step of creating a financial forecast actually happens after the job is complete. Review the numbers you projected and compare them to the actual numbers of the job.

Step 8: Do a postmortem on each project.

The most important procedure involving an estimate, budget, or projection, is to *compare* your actual results to your estimate. Investigate deviations from a plan and, if necessary, implement corrective actions or revisions to future periods. This is called job costing.

The elements of job costing are:

- Integrate your budget plan with the accounting records so that variances are isolated.
- Direct cost variances
  - These costs create the most volume, so you'll need good forms, procedures, or job cost systems.
  - Compare your actual costs to your budgets
  - Justify variances before paying invoices.
- Usual variances from budget and actual
  - Estimating errors
  - Change orders not on estimates
  - Sales concessions
  - Site conditions
  - Vandalism
  - Price increases

■ Measure performance and progress and help your people achieve their goals
  • Cost/profit ratios
  • Timeliness
  • Quality
  • Quantity of work done

By analyzing your cash flow, you will be able to predict, in advance, your seasonal fluctuations of cash. Use this information to establish alternate sources of cash flow and become a better deal maker. It should be noted that good feedback forms and accounting systems can help reach conclusions within minutes.

We've walked you through working in Excel and creating and setting up your financial forecast, as well as preparing your financial package for investors. There are still many permutations of forecasts left to discuss. Over the next two chapters we will introduce you to working with other amortizing debt, modeling projects with multiple phases and some advanced concepts that you may use if your projections are more complicated.

Working with Debt 14

We've talked about debt throughout this book. In this chapter, we'll concentrate on amortizing debt (debt paid off in equal payments). We'll build on this in Chapter 15 Advanced Concepts to create a projection for an income-producing project.

Analyzing Debt

When creating a projection, you may need to analyze debt which will be repaid in whole or in part during the forecast period. Therefore, all periodic payments for debt will need to be included in the forecast.

Before there was a software program that did the calculations for us, we did amortizations by hand. This is a quick overview for those who have never done it manually. Understanding the concepts will make doing it in Excel far easier.

For each loan, do the following:

- List the principal, interest, term, and monthly payments.

- For Month 1: Principal balance owing × monthly interest rate = interest portion of monthly payment. Then, total monthly payment − interest payment = principal portion of monthly payment.

- For Month 2: Determine the new principal balance owed as of Month 2 by subtracting the Month 1 principal portion from the beginning principal balance. Then, use the same formula again.

    Example: Loan Principal = $50,000; Term = 5 years (60 months)
                      Interest Rate = 12% (1.0% per month)
                      Total Monthly Payment = $1,112.22 (principal and interest)

Table 14.1 A traditional amortization schedule

	(a) *Principal Balance Owing*	(b) *Monthly Interest Rate*	(c) *Interest Portion*	(d) *Total Monthly Loan Payment*	(e) *Principal Paid*
Month 1:	50,000.00	1.000%	500.00	1,112.22	612.22
Month 2:	49,387.78	1.000%	493.88	1,112.22	618.34
Month 3:	48,769.43	1.000%	487.69	1,112.22	593.54
Month 4:	and so on for the forecast period				

Here are the formulas for table 14.1:

■ Principal Balance Owing: (a) – (f) from previous month

■ Monthly Interest Rate: Interest rate/12

■ Interest Portion: (a) × (b). This is what we are trying to calculate right now.

■ Total Monthly Loan Payment: You would receive this from the lender.

■ Principal Paid: (d) – (c) Subtract the interest portion from the total monthly payment to find the principal payment.

Note: principal payments are found on the balance sheet not the income statement.

PMT function

Amortizing a loan will make use of the following Excel functions: PMT, IPMT and PPMT. In Chapter 2 More Power with Functions and Formulas we covered the PMT function. If you recall, the syntax for that function was:

$$=PMT(rate, nper, pv, [fv], [type])$$

I'd like to expand the earlier discussion by adding the following warning: Make sure that you are consistent about the units you use for specifying rate and nper. If you make monthly payments on a four-year loan at an annual interest rate of 12 percent, use 12%/12 for rate and 4*12 for nper. If you make annual payments on the same loan, use 12 percent for rate and 4 for nper.

IPMT function

IPMT returns the interest payment for a given period for an investment based on periodic, constant payments, and a constant interest rate. The syntax is as follows:

=IPMT(rate, per, nper, pv, [fv], [type])

The IPMT function syntax has the same arguments as PMT except that the value returned is the interest portion of the payment instead of the whole payment.

PPMT function

PPMT returns the payment on the principal for a given period for an investment based on periodic, constant payments and a constant interest rate. The syntax is as follows:

=PPMT(rate, per, nper, pv, [fv], [type])

The PPMT function syntax has the same arguments as PMT except that the value returned is the principal portion of the payment instead of the whole payment.

The value returned for IPMT plus the value returned for PPMT should equal the PMT.

Case 1: Straight Amortization

We will put these functions to work in Chapter 14_Working with Debt at www.nahb.org/financialforecasting. You will see that the five cases we will cover in this chapter already set up. We have included the detailed instructions here if you want to recreate this on your own. Our first case is a normal amortizing loan:

1) Set up the assumptions (fig 14.1).

- In cells A1:A4, enter the labels: *Principal, Interest, Term (mo),* and *PMT* respectively.

- In cells B2:B3, enter the values for each.

- In cell B4, use the following formula: =-PMT(B2/12,B3,B1). Note: the interest was entered at the annual rate, so divide by 12 to calculate the monthly payment.

Figure 14.1 The basic PMT function

	A	B
1	Principal:	50,000.00
2	Interest:	12%
3	Term (mo):	60
4	PMT:	1,112.22

2) Create the detailed amortization schedule.

- In cells A6:A11, enter the labels: Month (the applicable month of the projection, usually starts with one), Payments remaining (usually starts with the last month of the amortization period), Principal Balance Owing, Monthly Payment, Interest Payment, and Principal Payment.

- The first month of the projection is usually different than the second to the last. So in cell B6 enter *1* as that is the first month of the projection.

- In cell B7, the formula is: **=B3** where B3 is the term in months (if you used 5 years, you would have put in: **=B3*12**. It represents the number of payments remaining at the beginning of the period.

- In cell B8, the formula is: **=B1,** which is the principal amount.

- In cell B9, enter the formula: **=-PMT($B$2/12,B7,B8)**. Don't forget the minus sign in front of PMT.

- In cell B10, use the formula: **=-IPMT($B$2/12,1,B7,B8)**. **Copy** the formula over to the number of columns in the projection.

- In cell B11, use the formula: **=-PPMT($B$2/12,1,B7,B8)**. **Copy** the formula over to the number of columns in the projection.

- For period two, there are slight changes in the formulas. Cell C6 has the formula: **=B6+1,** which increments the month by 1. In this case, we are in month 2. **Copy** the formula to the number of columns in the projection period.

- In cell C7, enter the formula: **=B7-1,** which decreases the number of payments left to 59. **Copy** the formula over to the number of columns in the projection.

- In cell C8, use the formula: **=B8-B11**. which says that your principal owed from last month is decreased by the amount of the principal payment made last month.

- Lines 8, 9, and 10 are just copies from column B (adjusted automatically by Excel when you copied them over).

Note the minus sign on the formulas on lines 9, 10, and 11. It is imperative that you use them.

Figure 14.2 shows the first six months of the projection you just created.

Figure 14.2 The IPMT and PPMT functions

	A	B	C	D	E	F	G
6	Month:	1	2	3	4	5	6
7	Payments Remaining:	60	59	58	57	56	55
8	Principal Balance Owing:	50,000.00	49,387.78	48,769.43	48,144.90	47,514.13	46,877.05
9	Monthly Payment	1,112.22	1,112.22	1,112.22	1,112.22	1,112.22	1,112.22
10	Interest Payment	500.00	493.88	487.69	481.45	475.14	468.77
11	Principal Payment	612.22	618.34	624.53	630.77	637.08	643.45

To prove that the calculations are correct, note that the monthly payments (once recalculated) on line 9 are *always* the same. If they are not, you have an error in your formula.

Case 2: Interest-only Payments

Our second case includes interest-only for a period of some months before principal and interest payments are made. Using the same worksheet from Case 1, here are the detailed steps:

1) Set up the assumptions.

- In cells A14:A18, enter the labels: *Principal, Interest, Term (mo), Months of Interest Only,* and *Principal & Interest Start in Mo.,* respectively.

- In cells B14:B17, enter the values. Note: term includes all payments (the monthly payments and the payments that are for interest only).

- In cell B18, enter: **=B16-B17** (fig 14.3), which is the beginning payment for amortization.

Figure 14.3 The setup for interest-only payments

	A	B
13	Case 2: Interest only payments	
14	Principal:	50,000.00
15	Interest:	12%
16	Term (mo):	60
17	Months of Interest only:	5
18	Principal & Interest Start in Mo.:	55.00

2) Create the detailed amortization schedule.

- In cells A20:A26, enter the labels: *Month, Payments remaining, Principal Balance Owing, Monthly Payment, Interest Payment,* and *Principal Payment.*

- The first month of the projection is usually different than the second to the last. So in cell B20 enter *1* as that is the first month of the projection.

- In cell B21, the formula is: **=B16** where B16 is the term in months (if you used 5 years, you would have put in: **=B16*12**).

- In cell B22, the formula is: **=B14**, which is the principal amount.

- In cell B23, enter formula: **=IF(B21>$B$18,B22*$B$15/12,-PMT($B$15/12, B21,B22))**, which is the total payment amount. Don't forget the minus sign in front of PMT. The formula tells Excel that if the number of the payment is greater than the month in which the loan starts amortizing (which makes it an interest only payment), then mulitply the principal amount by the interest rate, otherwise if the loan is in the period in which amortization is happening, then calculate the monthly payment. **Copy** the formula over to the number of columns in the projection.

- In cell B24, enter the formula: **=IF(B21>$B$18,B22*$B$15/12,-IPMT ($B$15/12,1,B21,B22))** This is the interest portion of the payment. **Copy** the formula over to the number of columns in the projection.

- In cell B25, enter the formula: **=+B23-B24**, which is the principal portion of the payments. Notice I created a shortcut. In cell B11, I used the formula: **=-PPMT($B$2/12,1,B7,B8)** (Note: This formula is complex and redundant since the principal payment is always the difference between the total payment and the interest portion. It was included earlier to illustrate the use of the PPMT function.)

- For period two there are slight changes in the formulas. Cell C20 contains the formula: **=B20+1**, which increments the month by 1. In this case, we are in month 2. **Copy** the formula to the number of columns in the projection period.

- In cell C21, enter the formula: **=B21-1**, which decreases the number of payments left to 59. **Copy** the formula over to the number of columns in the projection.

- In cell C22, enter the formula: **=B22-B25**, which says that your principal owed from last month is decrease by the amount of the principal payment made last month.

- Lines 23, 24, and 25 are just copies from column B (adjusted automatically by Excel when you copied them over).

Figure 14.4 shows the first seven months of the projection you just created.

Figure 14.4 Amortization with interest only for a specified period of time

	A	B	C	D	E	F	G	H
20	Month	1	2	3	4	5	6	7
21	Payments remaining:	60	59	58	57	56	55	54
22	Principal Balance Owing	50,000.00	50,000.00	50,000.00	50,000.00	50,000.00	50,000.00	49,313.68
23	Monthly Payment	500.00	500.00	500.00	500.00	500.00	1,186.32	1,186.32
24	Interest Payment	500.00	500.00	500.00	500.00	500.00	500.00	493.14
25	Principal Payment	0.00	0.00	0.00	0.00	0.00	686.32	693.18

To prove that the calculations are correct, note that the monthly payments (once recalculated) on line 23 are *always* the same during the period of interest only and always the same during the amortization period. If they are not, you have an error in your formula.

Case 3: The loan doesn't start in the first period of the projection.

In the third case, the first payment is deferred to a future month, then interest only, and then principal and interest. By now, you will be seeing a pattern in the cases. I'll only explain that which is different. In the same worksheet, here are the detailed steps:

1) Set up the assumptions.

■ In cells A28:A33, enter the labels: *Principal, Interest, Term (mo), Month the Loan Begins, Months of Interest Only,* and *Principal & Interest Start in Mo.,* respectively.

■ In cells B28:B33, enter the corresponding values (fig 14.5).

■ In cell B33, enter the formula: =B30-B32, which is the beginning payment for amortization.

Figure 14.5 The shaded cells highlight the new changes for Case 3.

	A	B
27	Case 3: Loan Starting Date Different	
28	Principal:	50,000.00
29	Interest:	12%
30	Term (mo):	60
31	Month Loan Begins:	3
32	Months of Interest Only:	2
33	Principal & Interest Start in Mo.:	58

3) Create the detailed amortization schedule.

■ In cells A35:A41, enter the labels: *Month, Payments remaining, Additions (this is new), Principal Balance Owing, Monthly Payment, Interest Payment,* and *Principal Payment.*

■ The first month of the projection is usually different than the second to the last. So in cell B35 enter "1". In cell C35, enter the formula: **=B35+1**, which increases the month by 1. In this case, we are in month 2. **Copy** the formula to the number of columns in the projection period.

■ In cell B36, we need a more complicated formula: **=IF($B31=B35,$B30,0)**, which says that if the month is equal to the start month, put in the term of the loan, otherwise put in zero. In cell C36, we need to adjust the formula to: **=IF(C35=$B31,$B30,MAX(B36-1,0))**, which says that if the month is equal to the start month, put in the term of the loan, otherwise put in the maximum value of either the prior periods term of the loan less one payment or zero (the loan hasn't started yet). **Copy** the formula to the number of columns in the projection period.

■ In cell B37, we want to track when the addition of capital takes place. This will serve as a source of funds in a more complicated projection. The formula in cell B37 is: **=IF(B35=$B31,$B28,0)**, which says that if the current month equals the month the loan begins, then put in the principal borrowed, otherwise use zero. **Copy** the formula to the number of columns in the projection period.

■ In cell B38, the formula is: **=B37**, which is the incremental principal received, if any. In cell C38 the formula is: **=B38-B41+C37**, which is the amount of new additions plus the prior month's principal balance outstanding minus the prior month's payment applied to principal.

■ In cell B39, enter the formula: **=IF(B36=0,0,IF(B36>$B33,B38*$B$29/12,-PMT($B$29/12,B36,B38)))**, which says if the payments remaining are zero, then use zero, otherwise if the payments remaining (B36) are greater than the starting date for amortization, multiply the principal balance by the interest rate to calculate the interest only payment. If the other two conditions aren't true, then you are in the amortizing period and should calculate the principal and interest payment. **Copy** the formula over to the number of columns in the projection.

■ In cell B40, use the formula: **=B38*$B$29/12**, which is the interest portion of the payment. Note: We took another shortcut here and said to multiply the principal by the monthly interest. The objective is to always keep the formula as simple as possible. **Copy** the formula over to the number of columns in the projection.

■ In cell B41, enter the formula: **=B23-B24**, which is the principal portion of the payments. **Copy** the formula over to the number of columns in the projection.

Figure 14.6 shows the first six months of the projection you just created.

Figure 14.6 An amortization schedule where payments don't begin in the first month of the forecast

	A	B	C	D	E	F	G
35	Month	1	2	3	4	5	6
36	Payments remaining:	0	0	60	59	58	57
37	Additions	0.00	0.00	50,000.00	0.00	0.00	0.00
38	Principal Balance Owing:	0.00	0.00	50,000.00	50,000.00	50,000.00	49,359.71
39	Monthly Payment	0.00	0.00	500.00	500.00	1,140.29	1,140.29
40	Interest Portion:	0.00	0.00	500.00	500.00	500.00	493.60
41	Principal Payment	0.00	0.00	0.00	0.00	640.29	646.69

To prove that the calculations are correct, note that the monthly payments (once recalculated) on line 39 are *always* the same during the period of interest only and always the same during the amortization period. If they are not, you have an error in your formula.

Case 4: Same as Case 3 with a Balloon Payment

Our fourth case builds on the third case with the additional proviso that we will have a balloon payment. Once again, I'll only explain that which is different from the earlier cases. Using the same worksheet, here are the detailed steps:

1) Set up the assumptions.

■ In cells A44:A50, enter the labels: *Principal, Interest, Term (mo), Month Loan Begins, Months of Interest Only, Principal & Interest Start in Mo,* and *Month of Balloon,* respectively.

■ In cells B44:B48, enter the corresponding values as shown in figure 14.7.

■ In cell B49, use the formula: **=B46-B48**, which is the beginning payment for amortization.

■ In cell B50, enter the month the balloon payment is due.

Figure 14.7 The shaded cells highlight the new changes.

	A	B
43	Case 4: Balloon Payment	
44	Principal:	50,000.00
45	Interest:	12%
46	Term (mo):	60
47	Month Loan Begins:	3
48	Months of Interest Only:	2
49	Principal & Interest Start in Mo.:	58
50	Month of Balloon:	7

2) Create the detailed amortization schedule. (In this case, we need to add another test to see if the balloon payment is due.)

- In cells A52:A59, enter the labels: *Month, Payments remaining, Additions, Principal Balance Owing, Monthly Payment, Interest Payment,* and *Principal Payment.* This is exactly the same as Case 3.

- The first month of the projection is usually different than the second to the last. So in cell B52, enter *1* as that is the first month of the projection. In cell C52, enter the formula: **=B52+1,** which increases the month by 1. In this case, we are in month 2. **Copy** the formula to the number of columns in the projection period.

- In cell B53, enter the formula: **=IF($B47=B52,$B46,0),** which says that if the month is equal to the start month, put in the term of the loan, otherwise put in zero. In cell C53, we need to adjust the formula to: **=IF(C52=$B47,$B46,IF(C52>$B50,0,MAX(B53-1,0)))),** which is different from the last scenario. It says that if the month is equal to the start month, put in the term of the loan, otherwise if the month is greater than the month of the balloon, put in zero. Otherwise put in the maximum value of either the prior periods term of the loan less one payment or zero (the loan hasn't started yet). **Copy** the formula to the number of columns in the projection period.

- In cell B53, we want to track when the addition of capital takes place. This formula is identical to that of Case 3. This will serve as a source of funds in a more complicated projection. The formula in cell B53 is: **=IF(B52=$B47,$B44,0),** which says that if the current month equals the month the loan begins, then put in the principal borrowed otherwise use zero. **Copy** the formula to the number of columns in the projection period.

- In cell B55, the formula is: **=B54,** which is the incremental principal received, if any. In cell C55, enter the formula : **=B55-B58+C54,** which is the amount of new additions plus the prior month's principal balance outstanding minus the prior month's payment applied to principal. Again, this is the same logic as Case 3.

- In cell B56, enter the formula:

$$\text{=IF(B53=0,0,IF(B53>\$B49,B55*\$B\$45/12,}$$
$$\text{IF(\$B50=B52,B55*\$B\$45/12+B55,-PMT(\$B\$45/12,B53,B55)))))}$$

OK, let's break this down. There are 4 situations here (there are three IF statements): (1) if there are no payments due, (2) if we are in the interest only period, (3) if the month equals the month of the balloon, and (4) we are in the amortization period.

- Case 1: if there are on payments due then our monthly payment is zero.
- Case 2: If the payments remaining (B53) are greater than the payment in which principal and interest are due (B49) then we are in the interest-only

portion of the loan, so take the principal balance owing times the monthly interest rate (B55*$B$45/12).

- Case 3: if the month of the balloon (B50) equals the month we are in (B52) then we need to pay the interest due (same formula as Case 2 - **B55*$B$45/12**) plus the principal balance owing (B55). OR

- Case 4: (Note the cascading effect of these if statements, if it isn't Case 1 through 3 then we must be in the amortizing portion of the loan.) Determine the principal and interest payment (-**PMT($B$45/12,B53,B55**), our normal PMT formula. **Copy** the formula to the number of columns in the projection period.

■ In cell B57, enter the formula: =**B55*$B$45/12**, which is the interest portion of the payment.

■ In cell B58, enter the formula: =**B56-B57**, which is the principal portion of the payments. **Copy** the formula over to the number of columns in the projection.

Figure 14.8 shows the first eight months of the projection you just created. Month 8 is included to show that all the formulas produce a zero after the month of payoff without creating an error.

Figure 14.8 An amortization schedule with a balloon payment

	A	B	C	D	E	F	G	H	I
52	Month	1	2	3	4	5	6	7	8
53	Payments Remaining:	0	0	60	59	58	57	56	0
54	Additions	0.00	0.00	50,000.00	0.00	0.00	0.00	0.00	0.00
55	Principal Balance Owing:	0.00	0.00	50,000.00	50,000.00	50,000.00	49,359.71	48,713.02	0.00
56	Monthly Payment	0.00	0.00	500.00	500.00	1,140.29	1,140.29	49,200.15	0.00
57	Interest Portion:	0.00	0.00	500.00	500.00	500.00	493.60	487.13	0.00
58	Principal	0.00	0.00	0.00	0.00	640.29	646.69	48,713.02	0.00

To prove that the calculations are correct, note that the monthly payments (once recalculated) on line 23 are *always* the same during the period of interest only and always the same during the amortization period. The balloon payment (line 58) should be equal to the principal on line 55. If they are not, you have an error in your formula.

In this chapter, we dealt with period payments. In Chapter 15 Advanced Concepts, we will introduce you to more payment functions dealing with uneven amortization. You can see that loan amortization can get quite complicated depending on the nature of the loan. The purpose of this chapter was to show you some of the complications incumbent in a loan. Of course, the ways you can structure loans are limited only by your imagination.

Advanced Concepts 15

Let's take what we've learned and expand it to another level. Suppose you have multiple phases in a project and want to summarize them into an overall projection. This involves creating a new master worksheet, copying it for each phase, and summarizing the data. This chapter will cover the INDIRECT, CUMIPMT, and CUMPRINC commands.

Rental Properties

Tabs

In order to do this analysis, open Chapter 15_Advanced Concepts at www.nahb. org/financialforecasting. This file has all the information for this chapter included, but we will go over the step-by-step instructions so you can understand the concepts and can create this workbook from scratch. Let's look at the sheets you will need (fig 15.1).

Figure 15.1 Set up the following sheets in your new workbook.

| ◄ ◄ ► ►| | Assumptions | **Average Rent** | Summary | Equity Analysis | Beg | P1 | P2 | End | ☜ |

In order to do multi-phased projects, we need to create the phases. In this case, we are only going to use two phases: P1 and P2. These phases are preceded by a *Beg* tab (for beginning) and followed by an *End* tab (for end.) *Beg* and *End* are blank worksheets that surround the phases. These are blank so that we can enter summary formulas in the *Summary* page while at the same time inserting as many phases as we need without always changing formulas. Once again, we will create complicated formulas to allow for changing the projections quickly and minimizing errors.

Average Rent

Click on the *Average Rent* sheet as shown in figure 15.2. This should look familiar to you, as it is very similar to the *Avg Price & Costs* sheet in the construction projection template. Note there are detailed rental summaries for each phase of the project.

Figure 15.2 Calculating average rent

	A	B	C	D	E	F
1	Detailed Unit Information					
2	P1					
3				Number		Monthly
4	Unit Description		Size	Of Units	Rent/Sq. Ft	Price/Unit
5	3 bedroom - 2 baths		1,250	10	1.25	15,625
6	3 bedroom - 2.5 baths		1,350	20	1.25	33,750
7	3 bedroom - 3 baths		1,450	20	1.25	36,250
8	4 bedroom - 2.5 baths		1,650	10	1.25	20,625
9	x			0		0
10	x			0		0
11	x			0		0
12	x			0		0
13				--------		--------
14	Total			60		106,250
15	Avg.					1,771
16						
17	P2					
18				Number		Monthly
19	Unit Description		Size	Of Units	Rent/Sq. Ft	Price/Unit
20	3 bedroom - 2 baths		1,250	10	1.25	15,625
21	3 bedroom - 2.5 baths		1,350	25	1.25	42,188
22	3 bedroom - 3 baths		1,450	15	1.25	27,188
23	4 bedroom - 2.5 baths		1,650	5	1.25	10,313
24	x			0		0
25	x			0		0
26	x			0		0
27				0		0
28				--------		--------
29	Total			55		95,313
30	Avg.					1,733

Again, at this point, the formulas are basic, and you should be able to reproduce these formulas as well as the formatting.

Assumptions

Now click on the *Assumptions* sheet (fig 15.3). For this section, we are going to use a completely different set of assumptions than we did for construction projection, though there are significant similarities. The assumptions have been filled in, but with the knowledge you have now, you should be able to recreate this and link it easily.

Figure 15.3 Detailed *Assumptions* page

		A	B	C	D	E	F	G	H	I	J
1	1		Sample Company								
2	2		First Year of Projection	2014							
3	3										
4	4		**Project Assumptions**						**Participation Assumptions**		
5	5		Phase	P1	P2	P3	P4		Members:	Investors	GP
6	6		Name	Project 1	Project 2				Equity Contribution	90.0%	10.0%
7	7		Number of Units	60	55				Cash distributions before preferred & equity	80.0%	20.0%
8	8		Const. Start Date	Jan-14	Jun-15				Cash Distributions after equity & preferred	50.0%	50.0%
9	9		Months of Construction	7	6				Preferred Return on Cash Contributed	14.0%	
10	10		Month Ready	Aug-14	Dec-15						
11	11		Total Cost Per Unit	70,000	70,000						
12	12		Total Construction Costs	4,200,000	3,850,000						
13	13		Const. Costs Year 1	4,200,000	2,000,000						
14	14		Const. Costs Year 2	0	1,675,000						
15	15		Const. Costs Year 3	0	175,000						
16	16										
17	17										
18	18		**Rental Assumptions**						**Summary - ROI**		
19	19		Avg. Rental Income	1,771	1,733				Cash In From GP	360,000	
20	20		Vacancy Rates	4.0%	4.0%				Cash In From Investors	3,240,000	
21	21		Other Income	10,000	10,000				Total Cash Out to Investors	6,766,973	
22	22		Rent Increase Rates	0.5%	0.5%				Net Cash Generated	3,526,973	
23	23		Expense Growth Rates	1.0%	1.0%	80.0%			IRR	15.8%	
24	24		Property Insurance	2,000	2,000						
25	25		Property Taxes	1,250	1,250						
26	26		Other	2,500	2,500						
27	27		Management Fee	5.0%	5.0%						
28	28		Reserves	1,400	1,400						
29	29		Cash Contingency	100,000	100,000						
30	30		Safety Cash	50,000	50,000						
31	31										
32	32		**Debt Assumptions**								
33	33		Date Permanent Starts	Aug-14	Dec-15						
34	34		Loan To Costs	75.0%	75.0%						
35	35		Interest Rate	10.0%	10.0%						
36	36		Term In Months	180	180						
37	37		Principal Amount	3,150,000	2,887,500	0	0				
38	38		Monthly Payments	33,850	31,029	0	0				
39	39										
40	40		**Sales Assumptions**								
41	41		Year of Sale	6	9						
42	42		Cap Rate	10.0%	10.0%						
43	43		Sales Commission	10.0%	10.0%						

Summary of Differences

Note that column A contains row numbers. This will be important in the INDIRECT command. Row number one has the number "1" in it. From row 2 to the end of the assumptions, use the formula: **=OFFSET(A2,-1,0)+1**, which means take the value in the cell in the previous row (-1) and add 1. Use this so that if you insert a row, you can copy the formula and all numbers will adjust accordingly. The formula is copied into as many rows as there are in the *Assumptions* sheet. Another way to achieve the same end would be to use the command: "ROW()" The parentheses with nothing in it means take the current cell and return its row number.

Note that columns C:F contain the phase numbers. Often, the HLOOKUP command is used to access a particular phase. But that can fail for a number of reasons. We will use the INDIRECT command to save a lot of programming. On rows 7 and 19, the data will come from the *Average Rent* sheet. Line 10 is a calculated field.

The summary ROI information will be connected to the appropriate worksheet later.

INDIRECT function

Sometimes you don't want to hard code a cell reference into your spreadsheet, as you may want to refer to a cell whose value may change. The INDIRECT command references a cell by putting its address (or partial address) in another cell.

In figure 15.4, we want to reference row 3 but that row reference may change but we know we always want the value in column A. So, put the reference row in cell B1, and the value we want to get in cell A3 ("45"). We enter: =INDIRECT("A"&B1). The INDIRECT function takes a string of cell references (in this case, A and the value of B1), and returns the value at cell A3, which is 45.

Figure 15.4 Using the INDIRECT function

Let's say you want to access the number of units for Phase 1 from the *Assumptions* sheet. Create the following command:

=INDIRECT("Assumptions!"& "C"& 7).

This is the equivalent of saying: =Assumptions!C7 or get the value of cell C7 on the *Assumptions* page. Note the page with the explanation point and the C are all in quotes. That tells Excel to take those values literally. The fact that 7 is *not* in quotation marks indicates it is a dynamic row.

In cell A1 of the *P1* sheet, you can enter the column letter to look for on the *Assumptions* page:

=INDIRECT("Assumptions!"&$A$1&Assumptions!$A$7).

Finally, you know that both the rows and the columns could change, so reference the column you want to look for (*P1* page, cell A1) and the appropriate row which is located in the A column in row 7. Assume that the value in A1 is C. The formula is the equivalent of saying:

=Assumptions!C7.

Why not just enter "C7"? This complicated formula makes it dynamic. If row 7 becomes row 8 (because you inserted a row) then Excel would automatically change the formula to:

=INDIRECT("Assumptions!"&$A$1&Assumptions!$A$8).

No need for you to keep track of whether or not the references are valid. Excel does it for you. Why use cell A1 to put in the column number? So, you can make multiple copies of a worksheet. Then, you only have to change the column number in cell A1 and all the formulas adjust for the next phase.

I know this is confusing – that's why it's an advanced concept. Now let's apply the INDIRECT formula.

Phase 1

Click on the *P1* page in the document. Again, these are already filled in, but we are including the step-by-step instructions for you to create them on your own. Start by setting up the titles and periods as shown in figure 15.5.

Figure 15.5 Setting up the column headings

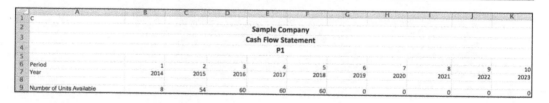

	A	B	C	D	E	F	G	H	I	J	K
1	C										
2						Sample Company					
3						Cash Flow Statement					
4						P1					
5											
6	Period				1	2	3	4	5	6	7	8	9	10
7	Year		2014	2015	2016	2017	2018	2019	2020	2021	2022	2023
8											
9	Number of Units Available		8	54	60	60	60	0	0	0	0	0

1) Set up the titles.

We will hide rows 1 and 6 before we set the print ranges. But they are used for computational purposes so for now leave them exposed.

- Let cell A1 equal C because you are going to reference the C column of the *Assumptions* page.
- In cell A2, enter the formula: **=Assumptions!$B$1**
- In cell A3, enter *Cash Flow Statement*.
- In cell A4, enter the formula: **=INDIRECT("Assumptions!"&$A$1&"$5")**, which means let cell A4 equal the value in Assumptions!C5, which is the phase name.

- Center cells A2:A4 over the applicable periods.

- In cell A6, enter *Period*. In cell B6, enter *1*, and in cell C6, enter the formula: **=B6+1**. **Copy** C6 for the applicable periods.

- In cell A7, enter *Year*. In cell B7, enter the formula: **=Assumptions!$C$2** and in cell C7 through the forecast period, use: **=B7+1**, which increases each year by one year.

2) Show how many equivalent units will be rented.

This is based on the weighted average of units outstanding. If we have 60 units and they can be rented for one year, then we have 60 equivalent units (think FTE's— full-time employees). If they can only be rented for half the year then you have 30 equivalent units (think part-time employee equals ½ FTE). Enter the equivalent FTU's (full-time equivalent units here). Use zero units if the complex has been sold, or not yet under construction.

The number of equivalent units to be rented can also be calculated another way. On Line 10 on the *Assumptions* page, we have the month of completion, which is a calculated field. We reference that calculation on line 47 by each phase. We then input how many units will come on board in that first period and how many will come on board each subsequent month. The inputs are shown in figure 15.6.

Figure 15.6 Step 1 in determining the absorption rate

	B	C	D	E	F
45	**Absorption**				
46		P1	P2	P3	P4
47	Occupancy Begins	Aug-14	Dec-15		
48	Beginning Units	10	10		
49	Monthly On-boarding	5	10		

We can then say 10 units are ready in the first month, and our absorption is 5 units per month. We can determine the percentage of units available during any given year by following the next set of steps.

- Cell B53 (fig 15.7) contains the formula: **=EOMONTH(DATE(C2,1,31),0)** and the format dictates the look of this column.

Figure 15.7 Monthly onboarding of units to be rented

	B	C	D	E	F	G
52	**Onboarding**					
53	Jan-14	0	0			2014
54	Feb-14	0	0			2014
55	Mar-14	0	0			2014
56	Apr-14	0	0			2014
57	May-14	0	0			2014
58	Jun-14	0	0			2014
59	Jul-14	0	0			2014
60	Aug-14	10	0			2014
61	Sep-14	15	0			2014
62	Oct-14	20	0			2014
63	Nov-14	25	0			2014
64	Dec-14	30	0			2014
65	Jan-15	35	0			2015
66	Feb-15	40	0			2015
67	Mar-15	45	0			2015
68	Apr-15	50	0			2015
69	May-15	55	0			2015
70	Jun-15	60	0			2015
71	Jul-15	60	0			2015
72	Aug-15	60	0			2015
73	Sep-15	60	0			2015
74	Oct-15	60	0			2015
75	Nov-15	60	0			2015
76	Dec-15	60	10			2015
77	Jan-16	60	20			2016
78	Feb-16	60	30			2016
79	Mar-16	60	40			2016
80	Apr-16	60	50			2016

- ■ Row 52:
  - Cell C53 contains the formula: **=IF($B53<C$47,0,IF($B53=C$47,C$48, MIN(C49+C$49,C$7)))**. This says:
    - ◊ Case 1: If the date is before construction is finished, there are zero units that can be rented.
    - ◊ Case 2: If the date in column B equals the date the first date units are available, then use the "Beginning Units" that are rented (this assumes that there are pre-start up rental activities).
    - ◊ Case 3: take the minimum of the units available (the previous months total plus the "Monthly On-Boarding Amount"). The MIN function assumes that we can't rent more units than we have.
  - Pay particular attention to the absolute references.
  - **Copy** this formula over the applicable columns that correspond to the phases.
  - In cell G53, enter the formula: **=YEAR(B53)**, which asks for the year. **Copy** this formula down to the applicable cells.

■ Row 54:

- Cell B54 contains the formula: **=EOMONTH(B53,1)**, which says take the previous date and move it one month. (Notice there are no absolute references in the formula.)

- Cell C54 contains the formula: **=IF($B54<C$47,0,IF($B54=C$47,C$48, MIN(C53+C$49,C$7)))**, which is almost the same as cell C53 except that there is a slight change in the MIN formula to the preceding cell plus this month's increment.

- **Copy** these formulas over to the appropriate columns and rows.

3) Determine the appropriate FTU's.

■ In row 90, enter "Percent of Units Ready for Occupancy" (fig 15.8).

Figure 15.8 Summary by year of units available for rental

	A	B	C	D
90	90	Percent of Units Ready for Occupancy		
91	91	2014	14%	0%
92	92	2015	90%	2%
93	93	2016	100%	88%

■ Row 91:

- Cell B91 contains the formula: =C2 which is the current year

- Cell C91 contains the formula: **=IF(C$7="","",IFERROR(SUMIF($G$53: $G$88,"="&$B91,C$53:C$88)/(C$7*12),0))**

This says:

◊ Case 1: if the number of units (C$7) is blank, show a blank as there are no units in this phase.

◊ Case 2: IFERROR – because we have a division we can get an error message if we try to divide by zero.

◊ Case 3, the SUMIF function adds the data in selected cells (C53:C88) when specific criteria are met (the year: ="&B91) equals the year on lines G53:G88.

◊ Divide Case 3 by the number of units (C7 which is 60 multiplied by 12, the total number of possible revenue "months").

◊ This gives you the percentage of rental rates to be realized in the first 3 years on a year-by-year basis.

◊ **Copy** this formula down 2 rows.

■ Row 92:

- B92 contains the formula: **=B91+1**, which adds one year to the beginning year. This is copied to B93.

4) Show the equivalent rental units on line 9.

■ The formula in cell B9 is: **=INDIRECT("Assumptions!"&$A$1&Assumptions! $A$7)*INDIRECT("Assumptions!"&$A$1&Assumptions!$A$91)* IF(B$6<INDIRECT("Assumptions!"&$A$1&Assumptions!$A$41),1,0)**. Let's break it down:

- Multiply the number of units **Assumptions!C7** (60 units) by the full-time equivalent usage, which we just calculated **Assumptions!C91** (14% used in relationship to a full year). Multiply that by 1 if the property is still owned by the owner or 0 if it has been sold.

5) Calculate the cash balance.

This is just like the construction projection we discussed in Chapter 4 Your Sales Forecast. You can look at lines 11 and 43 the *P1* sheet familiarize yourself with the formulas.

Receipts

For the sake of brevity, you should be able to put in row totals and column sub-totals as we discussed in Chapter 4. Also, I will go over the formulas when there is a new concept. Figure 15.9 shows the template for cash receipts:

Figure 15.9 The cash inflows for Phase 1

	A	B	C	D	E	F	G	H	I	J	K
13	Receipts:										
14	Permanent Loan	4,650,000	1,256,250	131,250	0	0	0	0	0	0	0
15	Rental Income	177,083	1,165,315	2,302,972	2,455,213	2,467,489	1,172,631	1,178,494	1,184,387	0	0
16	Vacancy	-7,083	-46,613	-92,119	-98,209	-98,700	-46,905	-47,140	-47,375	0	0
17	Other Income	20,000	20,100	20,201	20,302	20,403	10,253	10,304	10,355	0	0
18	Bulk Sale of Units	0	0	0	0	0	7,474,783	0	0	6,647,978	0
19											
20	Total Cash Receipts	4,840,000	1,138,802	2,231,053	2,377,306	2,389,192	8,610,762	1,141,658	1,147,367	6,647,978	0

Permanent Loan: The permanent loan formula in cell B14 is:

$$=INDIRECT("Assumptions!"\&\$A\$1\&Assumptions!\$A\$34)*INDIRECT$$
$$("Assumptions!"\&\$A\$1\&Assumptions!\$A\$12).$$

This takes the Loan to costs (Assumptions!C34) and multiplies it by the total costs (Assumptions C12).

Rental Income: This formula is tricky because we are going to use an inflation factor.

- The formula for B15 is:

    =+B$9*INDIRECT("Assumptions!"&$A$1&Assumptions!$A$19)*12*
    (1+INDIRECT("Assumptions!"&$A$1&Assumptions!$A$22))^(B$6-1).

    This multiplies number of units (B9) by the average rental income per unit per month (Assumptions!C19) then multiplies that by 12 to get the annual income.

- Multiply the revenue by the inflation rate (1) plus the inflation rate (Assumptions! C22), and use an exponent (the current period number less 1) to calculate the correct multiplier for inflation. So, the inflation rate is 1% per year. In year 2 it would be 1+.01, or 1.01. Then apply an exponent (year 2 minus 1, or 1) to that. For year 2, our inflation rate would be (1.01)1. For year 3 our multiplier would be (1.01)2 or 1.0201. And so forth. (Why not just 1.02? Because inflation compounds.)

- Also, notice the use of: **INDIRECT("Assumptions!"&$A$1&Assumptions! $A$19)**. The "Assumptions!" is in quotation marks, meaning it is text. The next part (&$A$1) refers to the phase number. (Why use &Assumptions!$A$19? If we used 19 only, that would be the correct reference. However, if we inserted a row on the Assumptions worksheet, it would change my row number and we need to be able to let Excel track the changes in more worksheets.)

Vacancy (cell B16) is just the vacancy rate times the current rent:

    =-INDIRECT("Assumptions!"&$A$1&Assumptions!$A$20)*B15

where B15 is the rent and Assumptions!C20 is the vacancy rate.

Other Income:

The formula in cell B17 is:

    =INDIRECT("Assumptions!"&$A$1&Assumptions!$A$21)*(1+INDIRECT
    ("Assumptions!"&$A$1&Assumptions!$A$22))^(B$6-1)
    *IF(B$6<INDIRECT("Assumptions!"&$A$1&Assumptions!$A$41),1,0)

This multiplies the other income from Assumptions!C21 by the inflation rate. If the current period is less than the year of sale (B$6<Assumptions!C41) multiply by 1, otherwise if it is the year of sale or later, multiply by 0 which negates any income in periods when you don't own the property.

Bulk Sale of Units: When you sell the property, you'll want to capitalize the net income stream. Thus divide the net operating income by the cap rate (*Assumptions* sheet, Line 42). So the formula in cells C18 and the adjacent columns through the end of the projection period (cell C18:K18) is:

$$=IF(C\$6=INDIRECT(\text{``Assumptions!''}\&\$A\$1\&Assumptions!$$
$$\$A\$41),(SUM(B15:B17)-SUM(B25:B29))/$$
$$INDIRECT(\text{``Assumptions!''}\&\$A\$1\&Assumptions!\$A\$42),0)$$

This says that if the current period (on row 6) equals the year of sale (Assumptions!C41) then subtract the operating income from the previous column which represents the previous year (SUM(B15:B17)) from the operating expenses from the previous year (SUM(B25:B29)) and divide that by the cap rate (Assumptions! C42), otherwise if it isn't the year of sale, use 0.

Note: a cap rate (or capitalization rate) is a number that you divide into the net operating income of the project to determine its market value.

Total Cash Receipts: This is just a simple sum formula of each column.

Disbursements

Again, we will give you the highlights of the formulas in this section of the worksheet (fig 15.10). Once we have reviewed this sheet, we will walk you through creating other phases and creating the summary sheet.

Figure 15.10 Cash outflows for Phase 1

	A	B	C	D	E	F	G	H	I	J	K
22	Disbursements										
23	Construction Costs	6,200,000	1,675,000	175,000							
24	Operating Expenses										
25	Property Insurance	16,667	110,258	221,022	236,969	239,339	115,611	116,767	117,935	0	0
26	Property Taxes	10,417	68,911	138,139	148,106	149,587	72,257	72,980	73,709	0	0
27	Other	20,833	137,823	276,277	296,212	299,174	144,514	145,959	147,419	0	0
28	Management Fee	8,500	56,494	112,765	121,421	123,249	59,157	60,048	60,951	0	0
29	Reserves	11,667	77,181	154,715	165,878	167,537	80,928	81,737	82,554	0	0
30	Debt Service	169,250	437,230	778,551	778,551	778,551	372,351	372,351	372,351	0	0
31	Sale of Units:										
32	Sales Costs on Bulk Sale	0	0	0	0	0	747,478	0	0	664,798	0
33	Loan Repayment on Bulk Sale	0	0	0	0	0	2,646,158	0	0	2,191,323	0
34											
35	Total Disbursements	6,437,334	2,562,898	1,856,468	1,747,138	1,757,437	4,238,455	849,841	854,919	2,856,121	0

Construction costs: This comes directly from the construction schedule in the Project Assumptions table on *Assumptions* page on rows 13:15.

■ For year one: =INDIRECT("Assumptions!"&$A$1&Assumptions!$A$13)

■ For year two: =INDIRECT("Assumptions!"&$A$1&Assumptions!$A$14)

■ For year three: =INDIRECT("Assumptions!"&$A$1&Assumptions!$A$15)

Operating Expenses: There are usually two types of operating expenses: per unit and a percentage of revenues. If the cost is per unit, then it will probably be greater than $1 per year and if it is a percent, the value will be greater than zero but less than or equal to one. That becomes the foundation for operating expense formulas. We will focus on the formulas in property insurance (line 25 - a constant dollar amount per unit) and management fees (line 28 - a percentage). The formulas will be the same, but the results quite different.

The formulas for operating expenses are quite complicated but should look somewhat familiar. For example, the formula below is for cell B25 (property insurance).

=IF(AND(INDIRECT("Assumptions!"&$A$1&Assumptions!$A24)>0,
INDIRECT("Assumptions!"&$A$1&Assumptions!$A24)<=1),INDIRECT
("Assumptions!"&$A$1&Assumptions!$A24)*SUM(B$15:B$16),INDIRECT
("Assumptions!"&$A$1&Assumptions!$A24)*B$9)*(1+INDIRECT
("Assumptions!"&$A$1&Assumptions!$A$23))^(B$6-1)

The first part of the IF statements tests whether or not the value on line 24 of the *Assumptions* page is a constant or a percentage. If the value on Assumptions!C24 is greater than zero or less than or equal to one, it is a percentage.

=AND(INDIRECT("Assumptions!"&$A$1&Assumptions!$A24)>0,
INDIRECT("Assumptions!"&$A$1&Assumptions!$A24)<=1)

If it is a percentage, multiply the percentage (Assumptions!C24) by the net effective income, which is gross potential rent minus the vacancy rate (SUM(B$15:B$16). Otherwise, multiply the dollar amount in Assumptions!C24 by the effective rented units in row 9 (which shows 0 if the units are not being rented or have been sold).

Now we get to inflation (the last component of the formula above):

"*(1+INDIRECT("Assumptions!"&$A$1&Assumptions!$A$23))^(B$6-1)"

This says to add the expense inflation rate (Assumptions!C23) and apply the applicable compounding rate (B$6-1).

This was a lot of formula to test if it is a percentage or a dollar amount. Apply it to either the effective rental income or the number of units being rented and inflating the answer by the applicable compounding rate.

CUMIPMT and CUMPRINC functions

We are going to skip line 30 (Debt Service of the *P1* sheet) for the moment to discuss interest and payments. We'll start with an example that illustrate how and when to use the CUMIPMT and CUMIPRINC functions. Let's say we are making payments over the course of one year but the payments are made on a monthly basis, which means that interest is compounding. We need to calculate how much principal and/or interest was paid during the year. There are multiple approaches to solving this problem, but the fastest method may be to use the CUMIPMT function to calculate the interest component and CUMPRINC to calculate the principal component.

Consider the worksheet shown in figure 15.11. In cell B8, the CUMIPMT function has been used to calculate the total interest paid from payments seven through eighteen. In cell B9, the CUMPRINC function has been used to calculate the total interest paid during the same time period.

15.11 Calculating principal and interest paid over multiple payments

	A	B
1	Principle	200,000
2	Interest	10%
3	Terms in Years	15
4	Monthly Payment	$2,149.21
5	Starting Payment Number	7
6	Ending Payment Number	18
7	Total Payments	$25,790.52
8	Total Interest Paid During Period	$19,417.53
9	Total Principal Paid During Period	$6,372.99
10	Proof - Total Payments	$25,790.52

The syntax for both is the same:

=CUMIPMT(Rate, Nper, Pv, Start_period, End_period, Type)

=CUMPRINC(Rate, Nper, Pv, Start_period, End_period, Type)

In our example, the formula reads:

=-CUMIPMT(B2/12,B3*12,B1,B5,B6,0)

=-CUMPRINC(B2/12,B3*12,B1,B5,B6,0)

Rate is the interest rate on the loan (divided by 12 to give a monthly rate), Nper is the number of payments over which the loan is amortized (multiply by 12 to give the number of months); Pv is the original principal value of the loan; Start_period is the beginning payment number for which total interest will be computed; End_period is the ending payment number for which total interest will be computed; and Type is a value of "0" or "1" to indicate whether loan payments occur at the end of the period (0) or the beginning of the period (1).

Line 4 uses the PMT formula to calculate the monthly payment. Line 7 is the monthly payments times 12 for one year. The starting payment number and the ending payment number are inclusive and contain 12 months of the loan. Line 10 is a proof that adds lines 8 and 9 to determine if they equal line 7.

Now back to sheet *P1* on the spreadsheet (fig 15.12).

Figure 15.12 Calculation of principal, interest and total debt payments by year for Phase 1

	A	B	C	D	E	F	G	H	I	J	K
45	Starting Payment Number	1	6	18	30	42	0	0	0	0	0
46	Ending Payment Number	5	17	29	41	53	0	0	0	0	0
47											
48	Interest	10%									
49	Term	180									
50	Principal	3,150,000									
51	Monthly Payments	33,850									
52	Total Payments	169,250	406,201	406,201	406,201	406,201	0	0	0	0	0
53	Interest	130,611	306,656	296,232	284,717	271,996	0	0	0	0	0
54	Principal	38,639	99,545	109,969	121,484	134,205	0	0	0	0	0
55	Ending Loan	3,111,361	3,011,816	2,901,847	2,780,363	2,646,158	0	0	0	0	0
56	Proof	0	0	0	0	0	0	0	0	0	0

Starting Payment Number: The formula in line 45 is:

$$\text{=IF(B\$7<YEAR(INDIRECT(``Assumptions!''\&\$A\$1\&Assumptions!}$$
$$\text{\$A\$10)),0,IF(B\$7=YEAR(INDIRECT(``Assumptions!''}$$
$$\text{\&\$A\$1\&Assumptions!\$A\$10)),1,A46+1))}$$

This says that if the current year (line 7) is before the year the units are ready (Case 1), enter zero. Otherwise, if the current year equals the year the units are ready (Case 2 -Assumptions!A10) then 1 (to indicate that the first payment is being made), otherwise (Case 3) the prior end period plus 1.

Ending Payment Number: The formula in line 46 is:

$$\text{=IF(B\$7<YEAR(INDIRECT(``Assumptions!''\&\$A\$1\&Assumptions!}$$
$$\text{\$A\$10)),0,IF(B\$7=YEAR(INDIRECT(``Assumptions!''\&\$A\$1\&}$$
$$\text{Assumptions!\$A\$10)),13-MONTH(INDIRECT(``Assumptions!''\&\$A\$1\&}$$
$$\text{Assumptions!\$A\$10)),12+A46))*IF(B6<INDIRECT(``Assumptions!}$$
$$\text{''\&\$A\$1\&Assumptions!\$A\$41),1,0)}$$

This is another complicated formula until you break it down.

■ Case 1—if the current year (Row 7) is less than the year before the units are ready, enter 0

■ Case 2—if the current year equals the year the units are ready, enter the 13 months minus the month in which they are ready (MONTH(Assumptions! C10). The logic is that if it is finished in December (13 minus 12) leaves one month of payments.

■ Case 3—if it is a year after the year of completion, you have 12 months in the year and add that to the previous Ending Payment Number.

■ Case 4—we multiply this number by 1 if we haven't sold the units or 0 if the units have been sold. So if the period on line 6 is less than the year of sale, multiply by one, otherwise the units have been sold and we multiply by 0.

Line 48: =INDIRECT("Assumptions!"&$A$1&Assumptions!A$35), which is the applicable interest rate.

Line 49: =INDIRECT("Assumptions!"&$A$1&Assumptions!$A$36), which is the applicable term.

Line 50: =INDIRECT("Assumptions!"&$A$1&Assumptions!$A$37), which is the applicable borrowed amount.

Line 51: =INDIRECT("Assumptions!"&$A$1&Assumptions!$A$38), which is the applicable monthly payments.

Line 52: =IF(B46=0,0,(B46-B45+1)*$B$51), which says that if there are no ending payments, use 0, otherwise use the number of payments (which we increase by one as these are inclusive payments) times the monthly payments (note the absolute reference).

Line 53: =IF(B$46=0,0,-CUMIPMT($B$48/12,$B$49,$B$50,B$45,B$46,0)), which says that if there are no payments, use 0, otherwise calculate the monthly interest for the year.

Line 54: =IF(B$46=0,0,-CUMPRINC($B$48/12,$B$49,$B$50,B$45,B$46,0)), which says if there are no payments, use 0, otherwise calculate the monthly principal for the year.

Line 55 – Ending Principal Balance: We need this number to pay off the loan when the units are sold. The formula is: =+B50-B54-B33. Take the principal borrowed minus the current principal payment minus any bulk sale payments toward principal. This is for year one. The formula for year two and thereafter is: =B55-C54-C33.

Line 56: =B52-SUM(B53:B54) subtract the principal and interest payment from the total payments. The answer MUST be zero or you have a programming error.

Disbursements (Continued)

Let's continue with Disbursements.

Line 30 – Debt Service: =B52. This may be the simplest formula in a long time.

Line 31 – Sales Costs on Bulk Sale:

=INDIRECT("Assumptions!"&$A$1&Assumptions!$A$43)*B18

This says to multiply the sales percentage (Assumptions!C43) by the sales price (in B18).

Line 32 – Loan Repayment on Bulk Sale: In cell B32, enter zero and in C32 enter:

=IF(C$6=INDIRECT("Assumptions!"&$A$1&Assumptions!$A$41),B$55,0)

This says that in the year of sale, get the payoff the loan balance on the previous period line 55.

Line 35 summarizes all the disbursements.

Equity Contributions and Distributions

15.13 Net cash flow and calculation of funds needed and distributed

	A	B	C	D	E	F	G	H	I	J	K	L
37	Net Cash Flow for Year	-1,107,334	262,026	339,491	340,398	341,278	4,081,147	0	0	0	0	4,257,006
38												
39	Cash Excess (Shortage)	-1,107,334	454,692	389,491	390,398	391,278	4,131,147	0	0	0	0	
40	Funds Needed	1,300,000	0	0	0	0	0	0	0	0	0	1,300,000
41	Cash Distributions	0	-404,692	-339,491	-340,398	-341,278	-4,131,147	0	0	0	0	0
42												
43	Cash Balance - End of Month	192,666	50,000	50,000	50,000	50,000	0	0	0	0	0	

Line 37 – Net Cash Flow for Year: In cell B37 enter: =+C20-C35, which is the sum of all receipts minus the payments made during the year.

Line 39 – Cash Excess (Shortage): The formula is: =B11+B37, which is the beginning cash plus or minus the Net Cash Flow for Year.

Line 40 – Funds Needed: This is essentially the same as the construction projection. In cell B40, we want to make sure that we have enough funds to cover all negative cash flow.

■ The formula in cell B40 is:

=-ROUNDUP(SUMIF(B37:K37,"<0"),-5)+
INDIRECT("Assumptions!"&$A$1&Assumptions!$A$29)

This says to take the sum of all months where the cash flow is negative ("<0") and round it up to the nearest 10,000 and add the cash contingency (Assumptions!C29).

■ In cells C40 through the forecast period, the formula is:

=IF(C39<INDIRECT("Assumptions!"&$A$1&Assumptions!$A$30),
INDIRECT("Assumptions!"&$A$1&Assumptions!$A$30)-C39,0)
*IF(C$6<INDIRECT("Assumptions!"&$A$1&Assumptions!$A$41),1,0)

This says if C39 is less than the safety cash (Assumptions!C30) then determine the shortage by subtracting the cash available from the safety cash, otherwise 0.

■ But we also have to test if the project has been sold. Therefore, if the period is less than the sale date, multiply by 1, otherwise multiply by zero because the safety cash is no longer needed.

Line 41 – Cash Distributions: This is the most complicated formula. There are 5 phases to a project: preconstruction, construction, operational, year of sale, and subsequent periods. So to determine how much cash we can safely distribute, let's break this down by project phase. The total formula looks like this:

=IF(B7<=YEAR(INDIRECT("Assumptions!"&$A$1&Assumptions!$A$10)),0, IF(B$6=INDIRECT("Assumptions!"&$A$1&Assumptions!$A$41),-(B39+B40), -MAX(B39+B40-INDIRECT("Assumptions!"&$A$1&Assumptions!$A$30),0)))

This formula is overwhelming until we break it down.

■ Before construction is complete, we don't want to make any distributions. So if the year on line 7 is less than or equal to the year ready (Assumptions!C10), then we don't want to distribute any money.

■ If the current year (B$6) equals the year of sale (Assumptions!C41) then we will distribute all the money (minus the sum B39+B40, we use the minus sign to create a negative to represent the outflow of cash), otherwise subtract whichever is greater: the MAX. This says if there isn't enough cash to maintain the safety level (which would create a negative number), then use 0.

■ We don't have to worry about years after the sale because of a component of the formula in cell B6 and subsequent columns. If you look in cell B40, at the end of the formula you will see:

IF(B$6<INDIRECT("Assumptions!"&$A$1&Assumptions!$A$41),1,0)

The formula says that no safety cash is needed if it is the year of sale or after.
Notice the proof. In cell L37, the formula: **=SUM(B37:K37)** calculates the net cash flow from the project. In cell L40, the formula: **=SUM(B40:K40)** which adds all the cash inflows. In cell L41, the formula: **=+L37+L40+SUM(B41:K41)** is the net cash flow plus the cash outflow plus the sum of all distributions. This should equal zero if the programming is correct. Remember, always try to get a zero in a proof cell to prove the formulas. This is a great habit as your eyes and/or fatigue can create big errors in your logic.

Phasing your Project

The hard work is done. Due to the INDIRECT command, all we have to do to create phases is add a worksheet between the worksheets "Beg" and "End," change the value in cell A1, and we are done. Yes, it's that simple.

1) Go to the *P1* sheet and click on the **Select All** button (or press **Ctrl + A**).

2) Then hit the **Copy** icon (or press **Ctrl + C**).

3) Go to the *P2* sheet (for Phase 2).

   ■ Click the **Select All** button.

   ■ Click the Paste➔Paste Special as shown in figure 15.14.

15.14 The Paste Special button

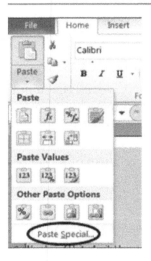

   ■ That pulls up the Paste Special selection screen (fig 15.15):

Figure 15.15 The Paste Special screen

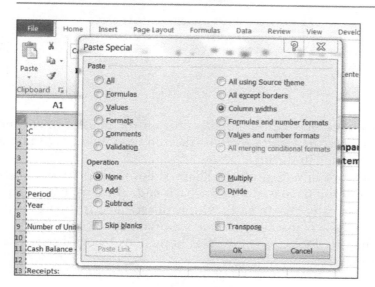

- Select Column widths and click **OK**.
- Finally, hit **Ctrl + C** and all the formulas will be copied from the *P1* page.

4) Type *D* into cell A1 as all the references are to column D on the *Assumptions* page.

Magically, everything now reflects Phase 2.

The Summary Page

For purposes of our equity analysis, you may want to consolidate all the phases into one summary page. This is easy, since we took the time to create our Phase 1 worksheet properly. All you need to do is copy Phase 1 to a summary sheet (outside of the *Beg* and *End* worksheets) and add all the phases together. There are many ways to do this, some simpler than others. Let's keep this simple as well.

1) Follow the steps in the previous section "Phasing your Project" to copy Phase 1 to the *Summary* sheet.

2) Enter: **=SUM(Beg:End!B9)** in cell B9, which copies the cells in B9 from the worksheet *Beg* through *End*. Remember, *Beg* and *End* are blank worksheets. Note the syntax: **=SUM(Beginning_Worksheet:Ending_Worksheet! Cell_reference)**. You can insert as many phases between the *Beg* and *End* pages as you like and the form will still work.

3) **Copy** cell B9 to the following ranges:

- B9:K9
- B14:K18
- B23:K30
- B32:K33
- B40:K41

Now, the spreadsheet has all the numbers for all the phases. Make sure you link rows 40 and 41 into the *Equity Analysis* sheet in rows 4 and 5. (Again see the formulas already included in the file).

We did a lot of work in setting up the Phase 1. But the more work you do on the front end, the less you have to do on the back end. Once we paid the price to get Phase 1 working, it was easy to add multiple phases, and to create a summary page. The equity analysis is just like the one we used in the construction projection. Again, take another look at the formulas in the Excel worksheets. The key is the INDIRECT command.

Final Thoughts Related to Forecasts

Dos and Don'ts of Projections

There are a lot of benefits to creating a projection. In fact, I create projections before I even write a business plan or a loan request. I want to see the financial viability of any project I (or my bank or investors) invest in. By looking closely at my assumptions, I can brainstorm with my staff and/or trusted advisors to determine whether or not the investment is plausible.

Once I complete my financial projections, I then complete a business plan or a financing request. You can request financing in the form of debt (i.e., from a bank) from investors or from parent companies. Remember, the purpose of the projection is to help tell a story and answer the four major questions:

- How much money do you need?
- When do you need it?
- How and when will you repay the money?
- What is the risk?

DO

- **Understand that a projection is critical to a successful outcome.** You wouldn't build a home without a blueprint, so why would you enter into a financial transaction without a plan? The financial projection is a blueprint of success.
- **Challenge your assumptions.** This book gave you suggestions for creating assumptions. These assumptions need to be in the projection as well as the

write up. It is important to include all of your assumptions in your proposal. Investors tend to stress numbers or text, so make sure the plan and the projection tell the same story.

- **Use numbers to answer who, what, where, why, and how much.** A financial projection contains details of a financial transaction and answers the aforementioned questions. Make sure that the projection makes sense from a macro and micro point of view. Remember, the language of business is numbers.

- **Summarize your numbers to be presented on the back of a napkin.** Financial projections may have thousands of cells with data. However, try to summarize all that data so that you can explain it on the back of a napkin. It helps investors, bankers, and other stakeholders focus on what's important.

- **Remember that a funding source must have information about your business in order to make a decision on whether or not to invest funds with you.** A potential funding source (either debt or equity) cannot make an informed decision on your request without adequate written information/documentation. A financing proposal is a tool that should be used to communicate critical aspects of your business to a potential lender. But, again the proposal must reinforce the numbers.

- **Make sure that your projection tells the "story" of your project/business.** Your projection should be able to stand alone without requiring additional explanation. Remember, whoever you present this projection to will become a future advocate to other people in their respective organizations. So clarity is imperative.

- **Make sure your projection presents a professional image.** Formatting and clarity within the projection are essential. While a loan proposal typically contains less information than a full business plan, it should still be presented in a professional manner.

- **Keep the audience in mind.** Typically, lenders see many proposals throughout the course of the year and work with a variety of business types. Most likely, a lender will not be an expert in your industry; therefore, you should explain any relevant technical/operational terms in detail.

- **Make sure that projected sales and expenses are reasonable.** Be conservative in estimating your revenues. Lenders may view over-inflated sales figures as unrealistic and unattainable. When projecting expenses, consider all possible costs and avoid underestimating.

- **Explain how the proposal relates to the financial projections.** Include a narrative explaining the assumptions you used to arrive at the dollar value of sales, expenses, etc. You must demonstrate that your numbers are reasonable.

- **Answer the key questions: who, what, where, when, how, why, and how much?** A quality loan proposal contains answers to each of these pointed questions. Make sure this information is clear and concise.

DON'T

- **Say that anyone can see that this project will work.** If a lender/investor says that they can't see your numbers, then you need to go back to the drawing board and make sure that the projection is self-explanatory. The projection does not need to be complex but it does need to be comprehensive. Some form of written narrative is usually recommended to explain the projection. Do not make your audience guess how your projection operates.

- **Create your projection in a vacuum.** Obtain the opinions of all stakeholders to make sure they agree with your assumptions and projections. Yes, even confer with non-financial people. If they can understand it, then your projection is doing its job.

- **Assume that your audience is as optimistic as you.** Listen to all input that you can get. You may have missed something that can be the difference between success and failure. In general, people are risk averse, so while it may be obvious to you that your business will succeed, you must get buy-in from your audience.

- **Assume that you can create a projection in a couple of hours.** It will take time to make the model fit your circumstance. In my whole career, I've never been able to drop the numbers into a projection without modifying the formulas. Making the projection reflect the anticipated sequence of events takes time!

Final Conclusion

There are more sources of capital than most people realize. From banks to private investors to insurance companies to partnerships with other companies to using your own money, each offers unique advantages. Regardless of the funding type you pursue, every source of capital will want to know the same thing: that their money will be used wisely. They want to know that loaning money to a business will help them achieve *their* objectives as much as it helps the business achieve its objectives. They want to know that they will get the money back. A good litmus test is to ask yourself, "Would I invest in this?"

By following the guidelines presented in this book, you are giving a potential investor (in the broadest definition of that word) the necessary information to make an investment decision. Moreover, by providing answers to questions before they are even asked, you are accomplishing something very important: your effort in creating a thorough, well-documented projection that shows responsibility, professionalism, and organization—the very traits that a potential investor wants to see. And when your source sees the information they want to see, you'll hear the words you want to hear: "Here's your check."

If you would like to ask the author questions or if you would like a review and/or help with your projection, email jkprager@backroommanagement.com. Thank you for purchasing this book; and we hope it helps you make great decisions toward your financial success.

Glossary

active cell. The cell with the bold black outline.

active sheet. The worksheet currently being worked on. It is indicated by the bold title on the sheet tab.

absolute reference. A cell reference in a formula that remains constant when copied into a different cell.

amortization. The paying off of debt in equal installments over time.

array. A list

assets. Things you own, although not necessarily paid for. They can be usually current or long-term.

balance sheet. A financial statement that gives a snapshot of the company's financial status at a given moment in time. It shows the assets, liabilities and equity.

budget. A process of estimating revenues and expenses before they occur.

cash flow. The movement of cash into or out of a business.

cash flow projection. A plan of cash receipts and cash expenditures for a specific period of time, usually in monthly increments.

cash flow statement. A financial statement that shows how changes in the balance sheet and income statement affected cash. This normally is presented in terms of operating, investing and financing activities.

costs of goods sold (COGS, also cost of sales). Costs incurred to produce and sell the products that are recognized as sales in your income statement. (*see also* variable costs)

equity. The value of a business to its owners after all obligations have been met. (*see also* net worth)

error trapping. Writing a formula that tells Excel that if it calculates to an error, it should populate the cell with a predefined value rather than any of Excel's default error messages.

fill handle. Used to fill in data automatically across a range of cells

financial statements. Documents that present the financial activities of a business; traditionally a balance sheet, profit and loss (income) statement, and a statement of cash flows.

fixed costs. Costs that typically don't change from accounting period to accounting period and will occur whether or not you have any jobs. (*see also* overhead)

formula bar. the bar at the top of the Excel window that you use to enter or edit values or formulas in cells or charts; It displays the constant value or formula stored in the active cell.

gross margin. The percentage of gross profit divided by gross sales.

gross profit. A company's revenue minus the cost of goods sold

hurdle rate. See *weighted cost of capital*

income statement. A financial statement showing the revenues and expenses of a company over a defined period of time.

internal rate of return (IRR). The discount rate at which the net present value of costs (cash outflows) equals the net present value of the benefits (cash inflows).

liabilities. Obligations a company owes to outside parties.

operating agreement. A formal understanding among members of a company that defines contributions, distributions, profit sharing ratios and a host of other issues involved in running the company

overhead. All expenses related to the sale of merchandise or services plus all other costs related to operating a business. Also called operating expenses.

principal. The amount of capital intially borrowed or invested, not taking into consideration any interest paid or accrued on it.

profit. Revenue earned by a company over and above all expenses.

pro forma. Forecasted financial statements that outline what the actual statements will show, as long as the assumptions they are based on hold true.

range. A group of cells in a worksheet that have been highlighted or selected.

relative reference. A cell reference in a formula that changes when copied into a different cell.

return on assets (ROA). How many dollars of earnings a company derives from each dollar of assets they control.

return on investment (ROI). The ratio of money gained or lost on an investment relative to the amount of money invested.

revenue. Income a company receives as a result of its business activities.

time value of money. The idea that one dollar today is worth more than one dollar in the future, due to its earning potential.

variable costs. Direct costs incurred to produce a product or service.

weighted cost of capital. The calculation of the cost of a company's capital where each type is weighted proportionately.

Index